GLENCOE

The American Journey

Unit Resources

Launching the Republic

The Federalist Era

The Jefferson Era

Growth and Expansion

McGraw Hill Glencoe

Book Organization

Glencoe offers resources that accompany *The American Journey* to expand, enrich, review, and assess every lesson you teach and for every student you teach. Now Glencoe has organized its many resources for the way you teach.

How This Book Is Organized

Each Unit Resources book is divided into unit-based resources and chapter-based resources. A description of each of the many unit and chapter activities available to you in this book can be found on page v.

All unit-based resources appear at the beginning. Although you may choose to use the specific activities at any time during the course of unit study, Glencoe has placed these resources up front so that you can review your options.

Chapter-based resources follow the unit materials. These activities are directly tied to their chapter and/or section and should be used during the course of chapter study.

A Complete Answer Key

A complete answer key appears at the back of this book. This answer key includes answers for all activities in this book in the order in which the activities appear.

The *McGraw-Hill* Companies

Mc Graw Hill Glencoe

Send all inquiries to:
Glencoe/McGraw-Hill
8787 Orion Place
Columbus, OH 43240-4027

ISBN: 978-0-07-880598-1
MHID: 0-07-880598-8

Printed in the United States of America.

1 2 3 4 5 6 024 12 11 10 09 08

Table of Contents

Launching the Republic

The Federalist Era

The Jefferson Era

Growth and Expansion

To the Teacher

The American Journey Classroom Resources

Glencoe's Unit Resources are packed with activities for the varying needs of students. Included are the following activities:

Citizenship and Decision-Making Activities

These activities are designed to involve students in grassroots community projects. These service learning projects help students understand how history affects their own lives on a daily basis.

Economics and History Activities

These interdisciplinary activities give students an understanding of the impact of economics on history. Applied to current situations, students are familiarized with economic terms and principles.

Reading Skills Activities

These reinforcement activities correspond to the reading skill lessons presented in each unit opener of the student textbook. The activities allow students to gain additional practice at such reading skills as monitoring, making inferences, and summarizing.

American Literature Readings

These readings provide students with the opportunity to read literature by or about people who lived during different historical periods. Each selection is preceded by background information and a guided reading suggestion, and followed by comprehension and critical thinking questions.

Enrichment Activities

These activities introduce students to challenging content that is related to the information in the student textbook. Enrichment activities help students develop a broader and deeper understanding of history and the community.

Interpreting Political Cartoons

These activities provide students with the opportunity to explore history through serious fun called satire. Students will analyze the cartoons for various methods used in revealing satire such as caricature, symbolism, metaphor, irony, sarcasm, and stereotyping.

Content Vocabulary Activities

These review and reinforcement activities help students master unfamiliar content terms used in the student textbook. The worksheets provide visual and kinesthetic reinforcement of vocabulary words.

Academic Vocabulary Activities

Knowledge of academic terms can significantly boost students' comprehension of academic texts. These activities teach word parts, word relationships, grammar, and other lexical information about academic terms.

Primary Source Readings

These activities allow students to "see" history through the eyes of those who witnessed events and participated in cultural movements. Each selection is preceded by an introduction and a guided reading suggestion and is followed by questions that require students to analyze and interpret the material.

Writing Skills Activities

These activities help students develop and practice writing skills. Skills such as brainstorming, outlining, learning sentence structures, using sensory details, and writing essays are applied to historical concepts.

Social Studies Skills Activities

These activities allow students to practice their critical thinking and social studies skills. At times, activities extend information in the text and can also apply to real world situations. These activities will help students develop skills needed to understand new situations and content.

Differentiated Instruction Activities

These activities give you an opportunity to differentiate your instruction, addressing the different types of learners in your classroom. Teaching strategies address these differentiated learning styles: English Language Learners, Advanced Learners, Below Grade Level, Logical/Mathematical, Verbal/Linguistic, Visual/Spatial, Kinesthetic, Auditory/Musical, Interpersonal, and Intrapersonal.

Critical Thinking Skills Activities

Critical thinking skills are important to students because they provide the tools to live and work in an ever-changing world. These activities show students how to use information to make judgments, develop their own ideas, and apply what they have learned to new situations.

Geography and History Activities

These activities provide students with the opportunity to analyze and interpret historical maps. Students are required to practice using geography skills as an aid to understanding history.

Linking Past and Present Activities

These activities help students recognize the link between the past and the present and understand how the past relates to the present. For example, exploring the changes in information technology from the printing press to computerized desktop publishing will help students realize the past is a prologue to what is present in today's world.

Time Line Activities

These activities reinforce the dates of major events in world history and help students learn the chronological order of those events. Students also see how events occur concurrently in different parts of the world and/or are interrelated.

School-to-Home Connection Activities

These activities contain information and activities that students and their families/caregivers can do at home to reinforce an understanding of geography. They are intended to give parents easy materials to help their children with chapter lessons.

Reteaching Activities

These activities may be used for remediation or reinforcement. A variety of activities enable students to visualize the connections among facts in their textbook. Graphs, charts, lists, tables, and concept maps are among the many types of graphic organizers used.

Guided Reading Activities

These activities focus attention on key information and enable students to make appropriate connections among the facts they encounter in the student textbook. They also provide help for students who are having difficulty comprehending the textbook or who would benefit from a review of the material.

Launching the Republic

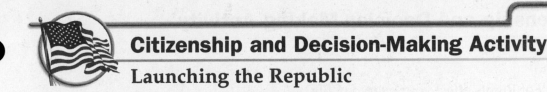

Citizenship and Decision-Making Activity
Launching the Republic

Get to Know Your Bill of Rights

Why It Matters

Most people in the United States would not like it if a government official told them that they could not meet with a group of friends to express their opinion on an issue. However, many people cannot explain why they have a right to do so. As a citizen, you need to understand your rights so you can protect them.

Background

The Bill of Rights is a list of 10 amendments that protect the individual rights of U.S. citizens. These rights grew from the concept of popular sovereignty, or the belief that the government gets its power from the consent of the people it governs. The Bill of Rights was not part of the original Constitution. In 1789 Congress created 12 amendments to the Constitution, 10 of which became the Bill of Rights.

Questions to Consider

Directions: Answer the questions below on a separate sheet of paper.

1. **Expressing** Which right from the Bill of Rights do you believe is most important?

2. **Making Decisions** Which rights affect you directly?

3. **Evaluating** How would your life be different if you did not have these rights?

> ### Did You Know?
> Two of the original 12 amendments were not ratified in 1789. One amendment defined the size of a congressional district. The other established pay raises for representatives. This latter amendment later became the Twenty-seventh Amendment to the Constitution in 1992.

Your Task

Take an active part in creating a school environment that is safe, positive, and respectful of diversity and differences.

Citizenship and Decision-Making Activity (continued)

How to Do It

How does the Bill of Rights affect your everyday life?

1. Form a group with one or two classmates and research a community, state, or federal issue by studying the local paper or doing research at the library. Choose an issue that is related to one of the first 10 amendments.

2. Form an opinion about the issue, either pro or con. On a separate sheet of paper, fill out a chart like the one below to help organize your thoughts, ideas, and facts about the issue.

3. Write a one-page editorial about the issue and submit it to your local newspaper.

Title of Editorial _____
Issue: _____
Opinion Expressed in the Editorial: _____ _____
Facts that Support the Opinion: _____ _____ _____

Follow-Up

Form a committee that includes students and teachers to study a local issue that affects students. Determine what students at your school can do to help.

Self-Assessment Checklist

Assess your editorial using the checklist below:

- [ ] We chose an appropriate issue.
- [ ] We stated our opinion about the issue.
- [ ] We found three facts that supported our opinion.
- [ ] We submitted our editorial to a local paper.

Unit

Economics and History Activity

Launching the Republic

Government's Role in the Economy

In his first Inaugural Address in 1801, Thomas Jefferson expressed his beliefs concerning the role of government:

> What more is necessary to make us a happy and prosperous people? Still one thing more . . . a wise and frugal government, which shall restrain men from injuring one another, which shall leave them otherwise free to regulate their own pursuits of industry and improvement, and shall not take from labor the bread it has earned.

Jefferson was expressing an economic policy called laissez-faire. In French, this phrase means "let (people) do (as they choose)." This idea became widely known when Scottish economist Adam Smith published his landmark book *The Wealth of Nations* (1776). In it, Smith explained and defended the laissez-faire philosophy. He argued that an economy will do best if government does not interfere. If left to pursue their own self-interest, individuals will naturally act in ways that will benefit society. To make a profit, businesspeople will provide products that consumers want to buy. Competition from other businesses offering similar products will keep prices low.

The laissez-faire philosophy is an underlying principle of capitalism, even today. However, as in Jefferson's time, economists and government leaders disagree about how much the government should get involved in the economy.

Government today plays many important roles in the economy. It passes laws to maintain fair competition and protect consumers from harm. It provides goods and services that benefit society as a whole, such as parks and a national military. It runs programs such as Social Security, Medicare, and Medicaid to help elderly people and those living in poverty. The chart below shows how the federal government spent its money in 2006.

Federal Spending, 2006

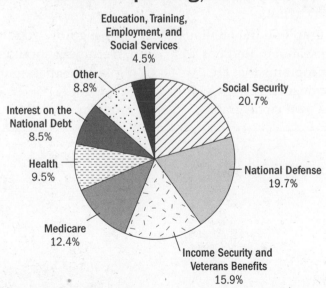

Education, Training, Employment, and Social Services 4.5%

Other 8.8%

Interest on the National Debt 8.5%

Health 9.5%

Medicare 12.4%

Social Security 20.7%

National Defense 19.7%

Income Security and Veterans Benefits 15.9%

⏳ Economics and History Activity (continued)

✓ Applying Economics to History

Directions: Use the information on the previous page to answer the following questions in the spaces provided.

1. **Summarizing** Using the quote from Jefferson's 1801 Inaugural Address, summarize in your own words three important points he made about the role of government.

_____

_____

_____

2. **Speculating** Based on Jefferson's quote, how do you think he would feel about a proposal to impose an income tax? Explain.

_____

_____

3. **Explaining** According to the laissez-faire philosophy, what role should government play in the economy?

_____

4. **Listing** Describe three roles the government plays in the economy today.

_____

_____

5. **Analyzing Visuals** According to the chart, the federal government spent the largest portion of your money on what program in 2006?

_____

6. **Calculating** The total budget in 2006 was $2,655 billion. How much did the federal government spend to pay the interest on the national debt that year?

_____

GOING FURTHER ▶ ▶▶▶

- Study the circle graph on the previous page. Conduct research to find out more about the programs that are included in the categories on the graph. Then create your own circle graph showing how you think the federal government should spend its money. Write a few paragraphs explaining why you would spend more or less on each program.

Reading Skills Activity

Launching the Republic

Summarizing Information

✓ Learning the Skill

When you summarize information, you focus on the main idea and the most important points. You reduce much information into a few well-chosen phrases that you can easily remember.

To summarize material effectively, use the following techniques:

- Read the material or look at the visual information.
- Identify and list the main ideas and important details.
- Organize the main ideas and details into a concise, brief explanation. Your summary should be in your own words.

✓ Practicing the Skill

Directions: Read the passage below about river travel. Then complete the graphic organizer on the next page with important details and a summary of the information.

River travel had definite advantages over wagon and horse travel. It was far more comfortable than traveling on bumpy roads. Pioneers could also load all their goods on river barges if they were heading downstream in the direction of the current.

River travel had two problems, however. The first problem related to the geography of the eastern United States. Most people and goods were heading west, but most major rivers in the region flowed in a north-south direction. Second, traveling upstream by barge against the current was extremely difficult and slow.

Steam engines were already being used in the 1780s and 1790s to power boats in quiet waters. Inventor James Rumsey equipped a small boat on the Potomac River with a steam engine. John Fitch, another inventor, built a steamboat that navigated the Delaware River. However, neither boat had enough power to withstand the strong currents and winds found in large rivers or open bodies of water.

In 1802 Robert Livingston, a political and business leader, hired Robert Fulton to develop a steamboat with a powerful engine. Livingston wanted the steamboat to carry cargo and passengers up the Hudson River from New York City to Albany.

In 1807 Fulton had his steamboat, the *Clermont,* ready for a trial. A newly designed engine powered the *Clermont*. The steamboat made the 150-mile trip from New York to Albany in the unheard of time of 32 hours. Using only sails, the trip would have taken four days.

Reading Skills Activity (continued)

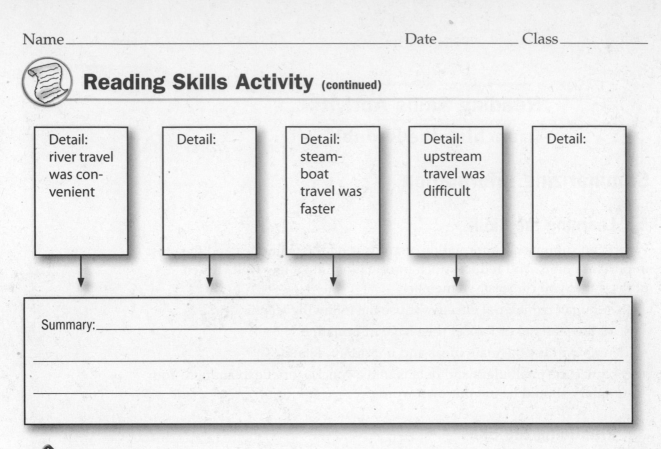

| Detail: river travel was convenient | Detail: | Detail: steam-boat travel was faster | Detail: upstream travel was difficult | Detail: |

Summary:_____

_____

_____

✓ Applying the Skill

Directions: Read the passage below about the development of canals. Then complete a graphic organizer like the one above with important details and a summary of the information.

Steamboats were a great improvement in transportation. However, their routes of travel depended on the existing river system. Steamboats could not effectively tie the eastern and western parts of the country together.

Business and government officials led by De Witt Clinton in New York came up with a plan to link New York City with the Great Lakes region. They would build a canal—an artificial waterway—across New York State. The canal would connect Albany on the Hudson River with Buffalo on Lake Erie.

Thousands of laborers, many of them Irish immigrants, worked on the construction of the 363-mile Erie Canal. Along the canal they built a series of locks—separate compartments where water levels were raised or lowered. Locks provided a way to raise and lower boats at places where canal levels changed.

After more than two years of digging, the Erie Canal opened on October 26, 1825. Clinton boarded a barge in Buffalo and journeyed on the canal to Albany. From there he headed down the Hudson River to New York City. As crowds cheered, the officials poured water from Lake Erie into the Atlantic. The East and Midwest were joined.

The success of the Erie Canal led to an explosion in canal building. By 1850 the United States had more than 3,600 miles of canals. Canals lowered the cost of shipping goods and they brought prosperity to the towns along their routes. Perhaps most important, they helped unite the growing country.

American Literature Reading

Launching the Republic

The Leatherstocking Tales

About the Selection

James Fenimore Cooper (1789–1851) was the first successful American novelist. *The Pioneers* was the first of five novels that became known as *The Leatherstocking Tales*. In this episode, Judge Marmaduke Temple, a merchant and landowner, speaks to his child Elizabeth about his part in the settlement of an area of New York State.

Guided Reading

As you read the story, notice how the author describes the countryside of New York State.

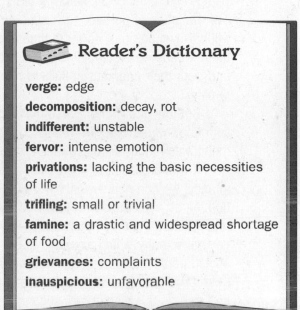

Reader's Dictionary

verge: edge

decomposition: decay, rot

indifferent: unstable

fervor: intense emotion

privations: lacking the basic necessities of life

trifling: small or trivial

famine: a drastic and widespread shortage of food

grievances: complaints

inauspicious: unfavorable

The Pioneers

The roads of Otsego . . . were, at the early days of our tale, but little better than wood-paths of unusual width. The high trees that were growing on the very **verge** of the wheel-tracks excluded the sun's rays. . . . The rich mold of vegetable **decomposition** that covered the whole county, to the depth of several inches, occasioned but an **indifferent** foundation for the footing of travelers. . . . Yet the riders, among these numerous obstructions . . . gave no demonstrations of uneasiness, as their horses . . . trotted with uncertain paces along their dark route. In many places, the marks on the trees were the only indications of a road.

"I have a remembrance of hearing you speak, sire, of your first visit to these woods. . . . Wild and unsettled as it may yet seem, it must have been a thousand times more dreary then. Will you repeat, dear sir, what you then thought of your enterprise?" This speech of Elizabeth . . . was uttered with the interested **fervor** of affection.

"Thou wast then young, my child, but must remember when I left thee and thy mother, to take my first survey of these uninhabited mountains," said Marmaduke. "But thou dost not feel all the secret motives that can urge a man to endure **privations** in order to accumulate wealth. In my case they have not been **trifling**, and God has been pleased to smile on my efforts. If I have encountered pain, **famine**, and disease, in accomplishing the settlement of this rough territory, I have not the misery of failure to add to the **grievances**."

American Literature Reading (continued)

The Pioneers (continued)

"Famine!" echoed Elizabeth; "I thought this was the land of abundance!"

"Even so, my child," said her father. "Those who look around them now, and see the loads of produce that issue out of every wild path in these mountains . . . will hardly credit that no more than five years have elapsed, since the tenants of these woods were compelled to eat the scanty fruits of the forest to sustain life, and, with their unpractised skill, to hunt the beasts as food for their starving families."

"But, my dear father," cried the wondering Elizabeth, "was there actual suffering? where were the beautiful and fertile vales of the Mohawk? could not they furnish food for your wants?"

"It was a season of scarcity. . . . Remember, my child, it was in our very infancy: we had neither mills, nor grain, nor roads, nor often clearings;—we had nothing of increase, but the mouths that were to be fed; for, even at that **inauspicious** moment, the restless spirit of emigration was not idle. Nay, the general scarcity, which extended to the east, tended to increase the number of adventurers. . . . No, Bess . . . he who hears of the settlement of a country, knows but little of the actual toil and suffering by which it is accomplished. Unimproved and wild as this district now seems to your eyes, what was it when I first entered the hills! . . . Not an opening was to be seen in the boundless forest. . . . I had met many deer, gliding through the woods, in my journey; but not the vestige of a man could I trace. . . . No clearing, no hut, none of the winding roads that are now to be seen, were there. Nothing but mountains rising back of mountains, and the valley. . . . Even the little Susquehanna was then hid, by the height and density of the forest."

Source: *The Pioneers,* reprinted in *The Norton Anthology of American Literature,* 6th ed., vol. B. W.W. Norton. 2003.

Literary Response and Analysis

Directions: Answer the following questions on a separate sheet of paper.

1. **Describing** How was the countryside different than it was when Marmaduke first explored it?

2. **Specifying** Why were people forced to hunt and gather food in what Elizabeth called the "land of abundance" five years before?

3. **Drawing Conclusions** According to Marmaduke, what two things might encourage pioneers to explore uninhabited frontiers?

Enrichment Activity

Launching the Republic

The United States Census

> Representation and direct Taxes shall be apportioned among the several States which may be included within this Union, according to their respective Numbers. . . . The actual Enumeration shall be made within three Years after the first Meeting of the Congress of the United States, and within every subsequent Term of ten Years, in such Manner as they shall by Law direct.
>
> — Article I, Section 2 of the Constitution of the United States

With this statement, the Founding Fathers created the U.S. census. The first census count, conducted in 1790, consisted of a door-to-door survey by U.S. marshals and their assistants. Their goal was to determine the number of free white males and females, the number of other free persons, and the number of enslaved people, in each household. The information was written on paper that the marshals furnished themselves, and the results were posted in public areas for all to inspect. The census information was used to ensure that every state had fair representation in the U.S. House of Representatives based on population.

Since that time, the U.S. Census Bureau has conducted more than 20 census counts. In later censuses, members of households were asked more questions, such as occupation, place of birth, and school enrollment. Census data is now used for many purposes, including redistricting, federal aid distribution, and environmental impact analysis.

Maps and the Census

In the late 1800s, the U.S. Census Bureau began using maps to present population, economic, and other data by geographic area. Since then, the Census Bureau's mapmaking has progressed from simple outline maps to electronic databases and computerized map output. The areas mapped not only include large geographic areas but also areas as small as city blocks.

Using maps, government workers and decision makers in private industry can more easily visualize census data. By comparing maps from different years, trends in population growth and migration can be seen. For example, the map on the next page, which is based on data from the 1790 census, shows that the population of the newly formed United States was concentrated along the East Coast. It also shows that Virginia had the largest population at that time.

Enrichment Activity (continued)

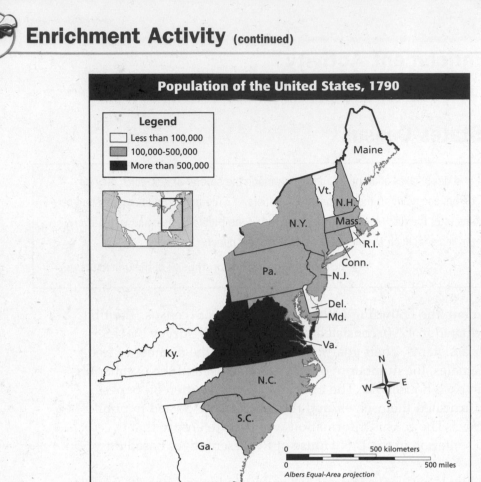

Population of the United States, 1790

Legend
- Less than 100,000
- 100,000-500,000
- More than 500,000

Maine, Vt., N.H., N.Y., Mass., R.I., Conn., N.J., Pa., Del., Md., Va., Ky., N.C., S.C., Ga.

0   500 kilometers
0   500 miles
Albers Equal-Area projection

Investigating the Censuses

Visit the Web site of the U.S. Census Bureau at www.census.gov. Research the population data from the censuses of 1800, 1810, and 1820. Use the data to create a series of population maps similar to the 1790 map above. Compare the maps to each other and to the 1790 map, and then write a brief essay explaining what the maps reveal about the increase in population and territorial expansion during this period.

Self-Assessment Checklist

Assess your maps and essay using the checklist below:

- ☐ I located census data for 1800, 1810, and 1820 online.
- ☐ I created maps that accurately represented the states and territories covered by the censuses.
- ☐ I used shading or patterns to indicate the population of each state or territory.
- ☐ I included a map key to explain the shading or symbols used.
- ☐ I determined trends in population and expansion based on the map data.
- ☐ I explained the trends in a well-organized essay.

Interpreting Political Cartoons

Launching the Republic

The Embargo Act of 1807

By 1807, the United States found itself in the middle of a dispute between the French and the British. U.S. ships bound for Europe were often stopped by the British, French, or both. Jefferson hoped to keep the United States neutral. He convinced Congress to pass the Embargo Act of 1807, which made it illegal for U.S. merchants to import or export goods. Although the embargo hurt Britain and France, it did more damage at home. New England felt the greatest blow because its economy depended on trade with foreign countries. In this tense environment, the Embargo Act became the subject of many cartoons, pro and con.

Directions: The cartoon on this page takes a strong stand on the Embargo Act. Study the cartoon, and then answer the questions that follow.

OGRABME, or, The American Snapping-turtle

Bettmann/CORBIS

Interpreting Political Cartoons (continued)

1. What in this cartoon represents the Embargo Act?

_____

_____

2. What does the man with the barrel represent? What is he trying to do?

_____

3. To which country does the ship belong? How do you know this? What is the ship waiting for?

_____

_____

Critical Thinking

4. Analyzing Information Americans had fun playing with the letters of the word *embargo*. What is the meaning of the statement of the smuggler, "Oh! This cursed Ograbme!"?

_____

_____

5. Making Generalizations Is the cartoonist in favor of or against the Embargo Act? Explain your answer.

_____

_____

6. Drawing Conclusions Like the smuggler in the cartoon, play with the words "Embargo Act." Create any words or statements that use the letters in "Embargo Act" and that might be the caption to a cartoon about the act. You can use any letters more than once. You do not need to use all the letters.

_____

_____

7. Evaluating Information According to this cartoon, the Embargo Act worked. How well did it work? Support your answer with facts and reasons.

_____

_____

Chapter Resources

The Federalist Era

Content Vocabulary Activity

The Federalist Era

Defining   DIRECTIONS: Select a term that matches each definition below. Write the correct term in the space provided.

precedent	tariff	sedition
cabinet	neutrality	caucus
national debt	impressment	alien
bond	partisan	nullify
unconstitutional	implied powers	states rights

1. *Definition:* to favor one side of an issue

   Term: _____

2. *Definition:* the department heads and attorney general set up by Congress

   Term: _____

3. *Definition:* maintaining a position of not taking sides in a conflict

   Term: _____

4. *Definition:* a meeting in which leaders choose their party's candidate for office

   Term: _____

5. *Definition:* a paper note promising to repay money in a certain amount of time

   Term: _____

6. *Definition:* an immigrant who lives in a country and is not a citizen

   Term: _____

7. *Definition:* to be inconsistent with the Constitution

   Term: _____

8. *Definition:* to force the military of one country to work for the military of an opposing country

   Term: _____

9. *Definition:* the principle that the powers of the federal government should be limited to those clearly assigned to it by the Constitution

   Term: _____

Content Vocabulary Activity (continued)

10. *Definition:* a tradition that helps shape a country or government

    Term: _____

11. *Definition:* to overturn something legally

    Term: _____

12. *Definition:* the amount a nation's government owes

    Term: _____

13. *Definition:* activities aimed at weakening an established government

    Term: _____

14. *Definition:* powers not expressly forbidden in the Constitution

    Term: _____

15. *Definition:* a tax on imports

    Term: _____

Chapter

Academic Vocabulary Activity
The Federalist Era

Academic Words in This Chapter

uniform	challenge	accumulate
resolve	maintain	principle

A. Word Meaning Activity: Identifying Synonyms and Antonyms

Directions: *Synonyms* are words with similar meanings, and antonyms are words with opposite meanings. Determine whether the following pairs of words or phrases are synonyms or antonyms. Place an "S" in the blank if the words are synonyms and an "A" in the blank if they are antonyms.

1. _____ uniform—consistent

2. _____ accumulate—waste

3. _____ challenge—demanding task

4. _____ maintain—preserve

5. _____ resolve—dispute

6. _____ principle—myth

B. Word Usage Activity: Using Words in Context

Directions: Write one vocabulary word from the box above on each line to complete the sentences.

1. Native American resistance to American expansion in the West was only

   one _____ facing the new government.

2. The _____ of states' rights declares that the powers of the federal government should be limited to those clearly assigned by the Constitution.

3. Congress members debated whether to have a(n) _____ , national legal system or leave rulings up to state courts.

4. The government had to show protesters it would use force to

   _____ order if necessary.

5. Government leaders worked hard to _____ disputes in order to avoid conflicts and wars.

6. Alexander Hamilton helped create a way to manage the debt the new

   nation was starting to _____ .

Academic Vocabulary Activity (continued)

C. Word Usage Activity: Understanding Words With Multiple Meanings

Directions: Some words like *uniform* have several meanings. Match the definitions to the sentences below. Write the correct letter in the spaces provided.

a. (n.) clothing worn by members of a group as a means of identification

b. (v.) to clothe with a uniform

c. (adj.) having the same form, manner, or degree

d. (adj.) consistent in conduct or opinion

e. (adj.) an unvaried appearance of surface, pattern, or color

_____ **1.** The builders used <u>uniform</u> marble storefronts for continuity in the downtown area.

_____ **2.** Judges try to rule with a <u>uniform</u> interpretation of the laws.

_____ **3.** The coaches voted to <u>uniform</u> their teams with commemorative armbands.

_____ **4.** The new <u>uniform</u> included each student's last name.

_____ **5.** The group followed <u>uniform</u> procedures for each meeting.

Primary Source Readings

The Federalist Era

A Federalist Promise Fulfilled

Interpreting the Source

As expressed in the Preamble to the Constitution, the purposes of a federal government are to "form a more perfect Union, establish Justice, insure domestic Tranquility, provide for the common defense, promote the general Welfare, and secure the Blessings of Liberty to ourselves and our Posterity. . . ." Despite these noble goals, Antifederalists were afraid that a federal government would harm individual, regional, and state liberties. One way Federalists responded to this fear, and ultimately procured the necessary votes to ratify the Constitution, was to promise to add amendments listing rights that would protect individuals and states from federal power—the Bill of Rights.

Guided Reading

As you read, think about what life would be like without these protections.

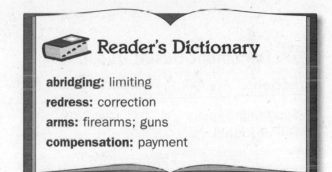

Reader's Dictionary

abridging: limiting

redress: correction

arms: firearms; guns

compensation: payment

Amendment I

Congress shall make no law respecting an establishment of religion, or prohibiting the free exercise thereof; or **abridging** the freedom of speech, or of the press; or the right of the people peaceably to assemble, and to petition the Government for a **redress** of grievances.

Amendment II

A well regulated Militia, being necessary to the security of a free State, the right of the people to keep and bear **Arms,** shall not be infringed.

Amendment III

No Soldier shall, in time of peace be quartered in any house, without the consent of the Owner, nor in time of war, but in a manner to be prescribed by law.

Amendment IV

The right of the people to be secure in their persons, houses, papers, and effects, against unreasonable searches and seizures, shall not be violated, and no Warrants shall issue, but upon probable cause, supported by Oath or affirmation, and particularly describing the place to be searched, and the persons or things to be seized.

Primary Source Readings (continued)

Amendment V

No person shall be held for a capital, or otherwise infamous crime, unless on presentment or indictment of a Grand Jury, except in cases arising in the land or naval forces, or in the Militia, when in actual service in time of War or public danger; nor shall any person be subject for the same offense to be twice put in jeopardy of life or limb; nor shall; be compelled in any criminal case to be a witness against himself, nor be deprived of life, liberty, or property, without due process of law; nor shall private property be taken for public use, without just **compensation.**

DBQ Document-Based Questions

Directions: Answer the questions below in the spaces provided.

1. **Specifying** Specify the "five freedoms" guaranteed by Amendment I of the Bill of Rights.

   _____

   _____

2. **Paraphrasing** Paraphrase why the federal government may not infringe on the right to bear arms.

   _____

   _____

3. **Listing** List the conditions stated in Amendment IV that are acceptable for issuing a warrant for arrest or search.

   _____

   _____

4. **Naming** Name the rights of a person accused of a crime.

   _____

   _____

5. **Making Generalizations** Which amendments reserve rights in general to the states and to the people?

   _____

   _____

Writing Skills Activity

The Federalist Era

Organizing and Displaying Information

✓ Learning the Skill

Suppose you are assigned to give a presentation about the national government. What will you talk about first? How can you make the information easy to understand? Organizing and displaying information on charts, maps, and graphs helps the viewer grasp the concepts presented.

Follow these steps to learn how to organize and display information:

- Research the information you need to present.
- Present the information in a logical way. For example, some information is best presented in chronological order, by the dates on which events occurred. Other information may be best presented by categories—discussing related items in one category, and the items related in another category.
- Choose the method that best shows the material visually. For example, a time line or graph shows information sequentially or how it changes over time. A chart or table allows you to group related items together by category.

✓ Practicing the Skill

Directions: Read the passages "Political Parties Emerge," "Views of the Constitution," and "The People's Role" in your textbook. Then complete the chart below with information about the first political parties.

Political Parties	
Federalists	**Democratic-Republicans**
• Rule by wealthy class • Strong federal government • _____ • Loose interpretation of the Constitution • _____ • National bank • _____ • Led by: _____	• Rule by the people • _____ • Emphasis on agriculture • _____ • _____ • French alliance • _____ • Free trade • Led by: _____

Name_____ Date_____ Class_____

Writing Skills Activity (continued)

✓ Applying the Skill

Directions: Read the section on President John Adams in your textbook. Then, complete the following chart about the XYZ Affair. First, fill in the legislation, and then explain why each piece of legislation was necessary and what it said.

XYZ Affair		
Legislation	**Why it was necessary**	**What did it say**
1. _____ _____	_____ _____ _____	_____ _____ _____
2. _____ _____	_____ _____ _____	_____ _____ _____

Self-Assessment Checklist

Assess your chart using the checklist below:

☐ I chose appropriate legislation for the chart.

☐ I organized the chart logically.

☐ I included information from the entire reading selection.

☐ I checked my spelling and grammar.

Chapter

Social Studies Skills Activity

The Federalist Era

Analyzing Primary Sources

✓ Learning the Skill

Original records of events made by eyewitnesses are known as primary sources. They include letters, journals, autobiographies, legal documents, drawings, photographs, maps, and other objects made at the time.

To analyze primary sources, follow these steps:

- Determine the origin of the source, identify the source's author, and find out where it came from.
- Examine the data for the main idea or concept.
- Learn what the topic reveals about the source.

✓ Practicing the Skill

Directions: Federalists believed in a strong, centralized national government controlled by a few, and Republicans believed in a government led by ordinary people. Read the quote below from Alexander Hamilton, and then answer the questions that follow.

> "All communities divide themselves into the few and the many. The first are the rich and the well-born; the other the mass of the people . . . turbulent and changing, they seldom judge or determine right. Give therefore to the first class a distinct, permanent share in the government. They will check the unsteadiness of the second. . . . Nothing but a permanent body can check the imprudence of democracy. . . ."
>
> —Alexander Hamilton's speech to the Constitutional Convention concerning the United States Senate, 06/18/1787, quoted in the notes of Judge Robert Yates

1. **Identifying** What is the source of the speech?

_____

2. **Identifying** What is the main topic of the speech?

_____

3. **Analyzing** What is Hamilton's message to others attending the convention?

_____

_____

Social Studies Skills Activity (continued)

✓ Applying the Skill

Comparing and Contrasting   **DIRECTIONS:** Thomas Jefferson maintained that a republican form of government was in the best interest of the nation. Read the quote below, and then note the views he shared compared to those by Alexander Hamilton in the previous quote. Complete the Venn diagram based upon information in the excerpts. Then on separate piece of paper write a short summary explaining what you learned about the two views.

> "... And the whole is cemented by giving to every citizen, personally, a part in the administration of the public affairs. ... I have thrown out these [opinions] ... for consideration and correction; and their object is to secure self-government by the republicanism of our constitution, as well as by the spirit of the people; and to nourish and perpetuate that spirit. I am not among those who fear the people. They, and not the rich, are our dependence [source] for continued freedom."
>
> —Thomas Jefferson
> a letter to Samuel Kercheval, June 1816

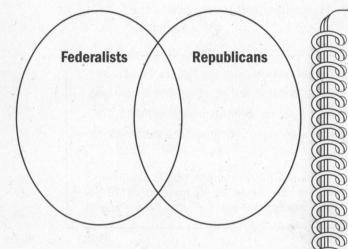

Federalists   Republicans

Self-Assessment Checklist

Assess your Venn diagram using the checklist below:

☐ I analyzed each primary source to see the views held by Federalists and Republicans.

☐ I analyzed the opinions of Hamilton and Jefferson.

☐ I completed the Venn diagram by showing the similarities and differences between the two statesmen.

☐ I summarized what I learned about the viewpoints.

Differentiated Instruction Activity
The Federalist Era

The Treaty of Greenville

In the late 1700s, the Northwest Territory was a region being disputed among Americans, Europeans, and Native Americans. In an effort to reduce British and Spanish influence in the territory, Washington signed treaties with the Native Americans that promised the land to them. When American settlers ignored the treaties and moved onto the land, the two sides began fighting.

In 1791 President Washington sent an army to stop the fighting, but the Native Americans won the battle and retained control of the Northwest Territory. When the Native Americans demanded that settlers move out of the territory north of the Ohio River, Washington sent General Anthony Wayne to confront them. In August 1794, General Wayne's troops decisively defeated the Native Americans during the Battle of Fallen Timbers.

On August 3, 1795, several Native American nations—including the Kaskaskia, Chippewa, Potawatomi, and Miami—signed the Treaty of Greenville with General Wayne. By signing the treaty, the Native Americans agreed to relinquish most of what is now Ohio to the United States. A boundary was now established between Native American lands and those lands that were open to settlement. Below is an excerpt from the treaty.

> To prevent any misunderstanding about the Indian lands relinquished by the United States in the fourth article, it is now explicitly declared, that the meaning of that relinquishment is this: the Indian tribes who have a right to those lands, are quietly to enjoy them, hunting, planting, and dwelling thereon, so long as they please, without any molestation from the United States; but when those tribes, or any of them, shall be disposed to sell their lands, or any part of them, they are to be sold only to the United States; and until such sale, the United States will protect all the said Indian tribes in the quiet enjoyment of their lands against all citizens of the United States, and against all other white persons who intrude upon the same. And the said Indian tribes again acknowledge themselves to be under the protection of the said United States, and no other power whatever.

Directions: Use the information from the treaty excerpt and your textbook to answer the following questions on a separate sheet of paper.

1. **Paraphrasing** Restate the main ideas of the excerpt in your own words.

2. **Making Predictions** How well do you think the U.S. government honored the terms of the treaty? Why do you think this?

Differentiated Instruction Activity (continued)

Teaching Strategies for Different Learning Styles

The following activities are ways the basic lesson can be modified to accommodate students' different learning styles.

English Language Learner (ELL)

Have students use a dictionary to find the meanings of the following words from the excerpt: *relinquished, explicitly, dwelling, molestation, disposed, intrude,* and *acknowledge.*

Gifted and Talented

Have students research the similarities and differences between the Treaty of Greenville and other treaties between the U.S. government and Native Americans. Then have them share their findings in a multi-media presentation.

Verbal/Linguistic; Interpersonal

Organize the class into three or four groups, and assign each group one of the Native American nations affected by the Treaty of Greenville. Then have each group use the library media center or Internet resources to learn more about that nation's language. Encourage students to create a dictionary of common terms that speakers may have used. The dictionary should include the spelling, a pronunciation guide, the related English word, and a definition. Students also may choose to illustrate some of the entries.

Verbal/Linguistic; Intrapersonal

Ask students to write a journal entry by a youth from the Miami nation regarding the treaty. Then have them write a journal entry by a settler in the Ohio River valley.

Logical/Mathematical

Assign students to create a time line of important historical events pertaining to the Northwest Territory from 1780 to the time of the Treaty of Greenville.

Visual/Spatial

Instruct students to create a map of the Northwest Territory at the time of the Treaty of Greenville. The map should indicate all Native American lands, show principal white settlements, and include the borders of modern-day states.

Kinesthetic

Have students research and create a replica of an artifact used by one of the Native American nations living in the Northwest Territory, such as a wampum belt. Invite students to explain the purpose of the artifact as they show their creations to the class.

Below Grade Level

Free writes engage students and explore their background knowledge. Bring to class several books or magazines that show draw-ings and illustrations of Native Americans from the Northwest Territory. Ask students to examine the illustrations closely without reading captions or words. Then have them write in their journals what they learned from the illustrations about Native American life. Emphasize that there are no wrong answers.

Chapter

Critical Thinking Skills Activity

The Federalist Era

Sequencing Information

✓ Learning the Skill

A sequence of events is the order in which events take place. Putting things in their proper sequence sometimes helps you see cause-and-effect relationships, or how one event causes another. Knowing the order in which events happen helps you understand their historical importance. Dates of events are important clues to look for as well. Transitional words like *first, then, finally, after,* and *later* are also clues to the order of events.

✓ Practicing the Skill

Directions: Read the following section on the new challenges facing Washington's administration in its early years. Then answering the questions that follow.

Taxation, westward expansion, and British and French pressures to involve the newly formed government in international conflicts were some of the early challenges facing the Washington administration. In 1791 westward expansion created conflict with Native Americans for control of the Northwest Territory. Two years later, Americans were becoming divided in their loyalties over the war between the British and French. Some Americans supported the British and some supported the French, while Washington worked for the country to remain neutral. Soon, attention was drawn back to the struggles at home. The farmers in Pennsylvania protested against the government's tax on whiskey, resulting in the Whiskey Rebellion in 1794. That same year, the British were urging Native Americans to destroy American settlements west of Appalachia in the hopes that the British would then be able to control the west. By 1795, the Treaty of Greenville was signed and the Native Americans agreed to surrender most of their land. Finally, Pinckney's Treaty, also signed in 1795, settled differences with Spain and gave Americans access to the Mississippi River and New Orleans.

1. **Sequencing** What are some of the clues that help you determine the sequence of events?

_____

_____

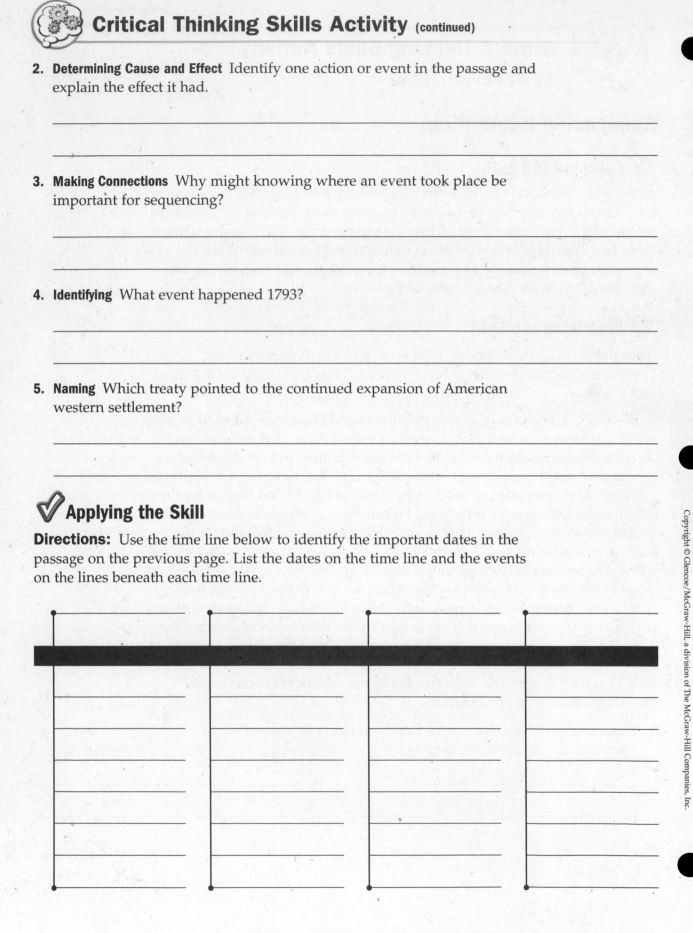

Critical Thinking Skills Activity (continued)

2. **Determining Cause and Effect** Identify one action or event in the passage and explain the effect it had.

_____

_____

3. **Making Connections** Why might knowing where an event took place be important for sequencing?

_____

_____

4. **Identifying** What event happened 1793?

_____

_____

5. **Naming** Which treaty pointed to the continued expansion of American western settlement?

_____

_____

✓ Applying the Skill

Directions: Use the time line below to identify the important dates in the passage on the previous page. List the dates on the time line and the events on the lines beneath each time line.

Geography and History Activity

The Federalist Era

Treaties and Forts of the Northwest Territory

The land north of the Ohio River, west of Pennsylvania, and east of the Mississippi River became part of the United States as a result of the Revolutionary War. Americans called the area the Northwest Territory.

Although the land was ceded to America by the British, much of it was already claimed by Native Americans. In the late 1780s, violence broke out in the Ohio country as American settlers, including illegal squatters, moved into areas claimed by Native Americans.

The Treaties

Arthur St. Clair, the governor of the Northwest Territory, attempted to establish a peaceful relationship between the settlers and the Native Americans. Two major efforts were made toward this goal. A series of proposed treaties were aimed at forcing Native Americans to give up their claims to much of the land. The Treaty of Fort McIntosh in 1785 set a boundary line between the United States and the Wyandot and Delaware nations. Many Native Americans ignored the treaty. The Treaty of Fort Harmar in 1789 restated the terms of the Treaty of Fort McIntosh.

The Forts

From 1778 to 1794, St. Clair also established forts in the Northwest Territory, mostly in what is present-day Ohio. These forts served multiple purposes. They were meant to control and to protect the settlers, as well as to provide staging areas for military attacks against the Native Americans. Staging areas are places where soldiers and military equipment are gathered before being sent out on military campaigns.

Many lives were lost on both sides during the battles with the Native Americans. The Battle of Fallen Timbers finally defeated the Native Americans. Disheartened and outnumbered, the chiefs signed the Treaty of Greenville in 1795. It required Native Americans to cede all but the northwestern corner of what is present-day Ohio to the Americans. The line dividing the land was called the Greenville Treaty Line.

Forts of the Northwest Territory

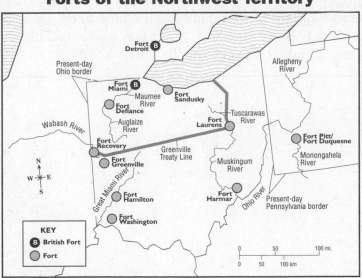

Geography and History Activity (continued)

✓ Applying Geography to History

Directions: Using the information on the previous page answer the following questions in the spaces provided.

1. **Explaining** What did Arthur St. Clair attempt to do through a series of treaties with Native Americans?

_____

_____

2. **Summarizing** What did the Treaty of Greenville accomplish?

_____

_____

3. **Drawing Conclusions** Why might the various forts have been built at their geographic locations?

_____

_____

_____

4. **Locating** Which forts belonged to the British?

_____

5. **Making Inferences** Why do you think the Native Americans ignored the Treaty of Fort McIntosh?

_____

_____

GOING FURTHER ▶ ▶▶▶

- What major present-day cities are built on or near the sites of Fort Detroit, Fort Sandusky, Fort Pitt, Fort Harmar, and Fort Washington? Conduct research on one of these forts. Explain how it became a city. Describe any ways the Fort influenced the city's development.

Chapter

Linking Past and Present Activity
The Federalist Era

The City of Washington, D.C.

THEN Major Pierre-Charles L'Enfant was a well-known French engineer and architect when President George Washington appointed him to design the U.S. capital in 1791. He surged ahead with an ambitious plan that included grand plazas, public squares, and parks connected by wide boulevards. L'Enfant, aided by African American Benjamin Banneker and others, did much of this work without authorization from his superiors. By 1792, President Washington dismissed him. L'Enfant's plans were set aside.

In 1901 the McMillan Park Commission revived L'Enfant's plans. Washington's streets are laid out like the spokes of wheels. The White House is at the center of one wheel; the Capitol is at the center of the other.

NOW Much has changed since L'Enfant designed a city in the wilderness more than 200 years ago. Hundreds of thousands of people live in the area. In 1800 about 3,000 people lived in Washington, D.C.; today it is home to nearly 600,000 people. Washington, D.C., is not only the seat of the federal government, it also attracts many tourists.

Every year thousands of people visit the capital. To many, the city is a monument to the ability of Americans to govern themselves.

With the development of the automobile, highways and expressways were built to handle the massive amount of traffic to, from, and through the nation's capital. In 1976 the capital's subway system began service. One of the Metro stations is L'Enfant Plaza.

L'Enfant's Plan

Directions: Answer the questions below on a separate sheet of paper.

1. **Explaining** Why did President Washington hire Pierre-Charles L'Enfant?

2. **Analyzing** Why was L'Enfant dismissed from his job?

3. **Drawing Conclusions** How have changes in transportation affected city planning in Washington, D.C.?

4. **Making Inferences** Why do you think the founders of the United States wanted the capital to be so grand?

5. **Evaluating** Why do people place so much importance on Washington, D.C.?

Time Line Activity

The Federalist Era

Problems With Britain and France

Directions: Use your textbook and the information in the time line to answer the questions in the spaces provided.

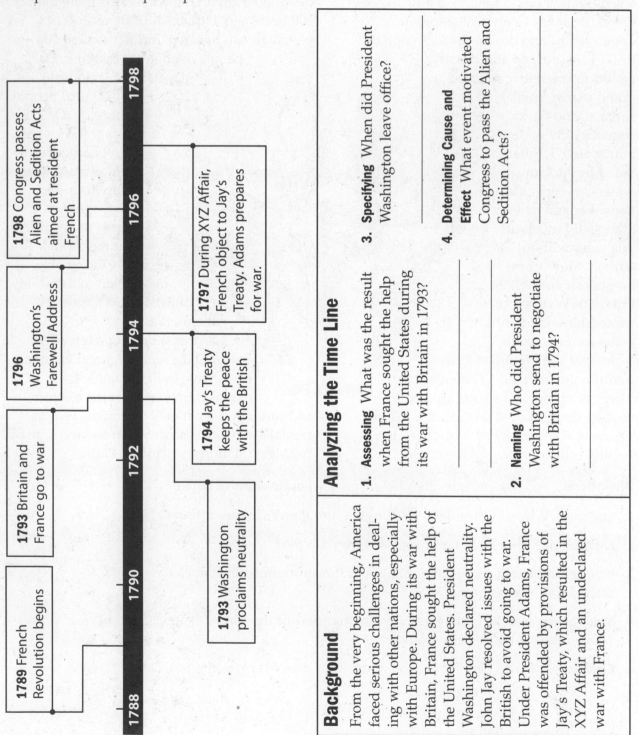

1798 Congress passes Alien and Sedition Acts aimed at resident French

1796 Washington's Farewell Address

1793 Britain and France go to war

1789 French Revolution begins

1797 During XYZ Affair, French object to Jay's Treaty. Adams prepares for war.

1794 Jay's Treaty keeps the peace with the British

1793 Washington proclaims neutrality

Analyzing the Time Line

Background

From the very beginning, America faced serious challenges in dealing with other nations, especially with Europe. During its war with Britain, France sought the help of the United States. President Washington declared neutrality. John Jay resolved issues with the British to avoid going to war. Under President Adams, France was offended by provisions of Jay's Treaty, which resulted in the XYZ Affair and an undeclared war with France.

1. **Assessing** What was the result when France sought the help from the United States during its war with Britain in 1793?

2. **Naming** Who did President Washington send to negotiate with Britain in 1794?

3. **Specifying** When did President Washington leave office?

4. **Determining Cause and Effect** What event motivated Congress to pass the Alien and Sedition Acts?

School-to-Home Connection Activity
The Federalist Era

What Do You Know?

Directions: Ask each other the following questions to see how much you know about the Federalist era.*

Student: Why was Washington, D.C., selected as the nation's new capital?

Partner's answer:

Student's answer:

Partner: What was Pinckney's Treaty?

Student: How did the British use the practice of impressment?

Partner's answer:

Student's answer:

Partner: What did the Virginia and Kentucky Resolutions claim?

*With your student, find answers to these questions in the student textbook.

School-to-Home Connection Activity (continued)

Understanding the Essential Questions

Directions: Rewrite each Essential Question as a statement. Then use your textbook to help you write details that support your statement in the graphic organizer provided.

Section 1 What were the precedents that Washington established as the first president of the United States?

Statement: _____

Executive Branch	Separation of Powers

Section 2 What challenges did the United States face during Washington's administration?

Statement: _____

Challenge	Washington's Response

Section 3 How did the Federalist and Republican Parties form, and on what issues did they disagree?

Statement: _____

	The Federalists	The Republicans
Who led the party?		
What type of government did they support?		
What was their view regarding implied powers?		
What was their view of the people's role?		

Reteaching Activity

The Federalist Era

Alexander Hamilton and Thomas Jefferson served as trusted advisors in President Washington's cabinet. Yet Hamilton and Jefferson held sharply opposing views on many important issues. As the election of 1796 approached, their supporters began to form the nation's first political parties: Federalists and Republicans. The growth of parties troubled President Washington. In his Farewell Address, Washington warned that parties could divide the nation.

Classifying Information   DIRECTIONS: In the chart below, decide whether each statement is true of Hamilton and the Federalists or Jefferson and the Republicans. Place a check mark (√) in the appropriate box.

	Hamilton and the Federalists	Jefferson and the Republicans
1. supported the principle of states' rights		
2. believed implied powers are only those powers that are "absolutely necessary" to carry out the expressed powers		
3. supported tariffs to protect American industries from foreign competition		
4. believed in a strong federal government		
5. supported a tax on whiskey that led to a rebellion in western Pennsylvania		
6. supported the Virginia and Kentucky Resolutions		
7. supported the Alien and Sedition Acts		
8. believed that only honest, educated men of property should hold public office		
9. favored banking and shipping interests		
10. supported limiting the power of the federal government to protect individual liberties		
11. believed implied powers justified the creation of a national bank		
12. believed in strict interpretation of the Constitution		
13. believed liberty can be safe only when ordinary people participate in government		

Section Resources

Guided Reading Activity

The Federalist Era

The First President

Reading Tip   Set goals as you read. For example, you may want to completely read and understand the information under the first main head before you move on. Take a short break after you accomplish each goal.

Answering Questions   **DIRECTIONS:** As you read the section, answer the questions below.

1. **Naming** What three departments did Congress establish in the executive branch of the government?

_____

2. **Explaining** What did the Judiciary Act of 1789 establish?

_____

3. **Analyzing** What is the purpose of the Bill of Rights?

_____

4. **Describing** What was Alexander Hamilton's plan "for the adequate support of public credit"?

_____

_____

5. **Defining** What is a bond?

_____

6. **Determining Cause and Effect** What did Hamilton promise Southern leaders in order to gain their support for his plan to pay off state debts?

_____

_____

7. **Identifying** What were two reasons for Jefferson and Madison's opposition to a national bank?

_____

_____

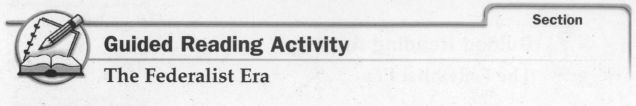

Guided Reading Activity

The Federalist Era

Early Challenges

Reading Tip

There are different ways to read. You skim when you preview material, or review before a test. You scan when you are looking for a particular main idea or name. You do in-depth reading when you read carefully to absorb new facts and ideas.

Filling in the Blanks   DIRECTIONS: Use your textbook to fill in the blanks using the words in the box. Some words may not be used.

Anthony Wayne	Pinckney's	Fallen Timbers
Jay's	Whiskey Rebellion	Arthur St. Clair
Mississippi	Wabash	impressment
Native Americans	neutrality	Spanish
French	New Orleans	Greenville

The new American government faced several challenges. An armed protest called the

(1) _____ involved violent attacks on government officials and destruction

of property. Although Washington signed treaties with the **(2)** _____, fighting

broke out between them and settlers in the West. General **(3)** _____ gained a

decisive victory over Native Americans in 1794 at the battle of **(4)** _____. As a

result, the United States acquired most of the land in present-day Ohio in the Treaty of

(5) _____.

European nations also challenged the United States in maintaining its **(6)** _____.

Americans were particularly angered by the British practice of **(7)** _____, in which

American sailors were forced into the British navy. This practice was not addressed in

(8) _____ Treaty, which did result in British withdrawal from American soil.

Differences with Spain were settled in 1795 with **(9)** _____ Treaty, giving

Americans free navigation of the **(10)** _____ River and the right to trade at

(11) _____.

Guided Reading Activity

The Federalist Era

The First Political Parties

Reading Tip

Are you confused by a part of a section? If so, reread the section and draw diagrams or jot down notes to help you. Then ask your teacher or a classmate for help.

Outlining   DIRECTIONS: Reading the section and completing the outline below will help you learn about the first political parties. Refer to your textbook to fill in the blanks.

I. Opposing Views

   A. _____ generally believed in a strong federal government and supported policies of the Washington administration.

   B. _____ wanted to limit the federal government's power and were followers of Jefferson and Madison.

   C. Jefferson and Madison believed in a(n) _____ interpretation of the Constitution.

   D. _____ supported representative government, and

   _____ wanted ordinary people to participate fully in government.

II. President John Adams

   A. The incident in which French agents demanded a bribe and a loan from the Americans became known as the _____.

   B. In order to protect the nation's security, Congress passed the

   _____ Acts.

   C. The Kentucky Resolutions suggested that states might

   _____ federal laws they considered unconstitutional.

   D. The _____ principle stated that the federal government's powers should be limited to those clearly assigned to it by the Constitution.

The Jefferson Era

Content Vocabulary Activity

The Jefferson Era

Word Scramble   **DIRECTIONS:** Unscramble the letters to find the term
from this chapter that completes each sentence below.

TAENRLU HRGIST   **1.** A nation that did not take sides and could sail the seas without fear of

conflict had _____.

GFIARET   **2.** A very fast warship used during the War of 1812 by the U.S. Navy was

a(n) _____.

DESECE   **3.** In order to create a "Northern Confederacy," Massachusetts Federalists

would first have had to _____ from the Union.

DJIUACLI VWEEIR   **4.** In *Marbury* v. *Madison*, three principles of _____ were
established to uphold the laws of the Constitution.

BTIRUET   **5.** For safe passage at sea, pirates demanded protection money, known as

_____, from other countries.

BREAMOG   **6.** The _____ Act in 1807 prohibited trade with other
countries.

SOTCEGAON GNAWO   **7.** In the early 1800s, a settler would use a(n) _____ to haul
household items westward.

MSSEIRPNMTE   **8.** The British Navy practiced _____ to force sailors who
deserted and were caught back into the navy.

AZEISLS-RFEIA   **9.** The French philosophy of _____ means "let people do as
they choose."

Content Vocabulary Activity (continued)

NOTANISLIMA 10. The loyalty felt toward the United States was known as

_____ .

TVPIRAERSE 11. Armed private ships, known as _____, captured numerous
British vessels.

MSOUCTS TIDUSE 12. During Jefferson's presidency, government funds would come only

from _____ , or taxes on imported goods.

Chapter

Academic Vocabulary Activity
The Jefferson Era

Academic Words in This Chapter

similar	authority	react	underestimate
conflict	purchase	restrict	goal

A. Word Meaning Activity: Identifying Synonyms

Directions: Read the underlined words below, as well as the four words or phrases next to them. Circle the word or phrase that is *most similar* in meaning to the underlined word as it is used in the chapter.

1. <u>similar</u>:   distinct, diverse, unique, alike

2. <u>conflict</u>:   harmony, disagreement, unity, coherence

3. <u>authority</u>:   power, weakness, disability, subjection

4. <u>purchase</u>:   loss, certificate, sale, land

5. <u>react</u>:   cause, respond, initiate, mimic

6. <u>restrict</u>:   permit, release, allow, limit

7. <u>underestimate</u>:   place a low value on, esteem, prize, assess too highly

8. <u>goal</u>:   step, question, objective, process

Academic Vocabulary Activity (continued)

B. Word Family Activity: Completing a Word Chart

Directions: A *noun* is a word that names a person, a place, a thing, or an idea. Examples include *president, Chicago, army,* and *slavery.* A *verb* is a word that is used to describe an action, an experience, or a state of being. Examples include *govern, attempt,* and *seem.* Sometimes the noun and verb have the same form. Fill in the chart below with the correct word forms.

Noun	Verb
1. authority	
2. reaction	
3.	conflicted
4. purchase	
5.	restrict
6.	underestimate
7. debate	

Primary Source Readings

The Jefferson Era

"One of the Most Interesting Scenes"

Interpreting the Source

Margaret Bayard Smith heard Thomas Jefferson deliver his first Inaugural Address in 1801. Although recently married to a man Jefferson hired to edit a Republican newspaper, Smith was raised on negative images of Republicans. Her father was a passionate Federalist. Jefferson, however, did not fit the negative images. After Smith met Jefferson, she considered him dignified, refined, and a proper gentleman. Margaret and her husband became leading figures in Washington's social life during Jefferson's administrations. The excerpt below is from a letter to Susan, Margaret's sister-in-law. It tells of hearing Jefferson's address to the nation.

Guided Reading

As you read, note the effect Jefferson's speech had on Smith and others.

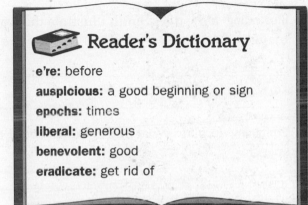

Reader's Dictionary

e're: before
auspicious: a good beginning or sign
epochs: times
liberal: generous
benevolent: good
eradicate: get rid of

Let me write to you my dear Susan, **e're** that glow of enthusiasm has fled, which now animates my feelings; let me congratulate not only you, but all my fellow citizens, on an event which will have so **auspicious** an influence on their political welfare. I have this morning witnessed one of the most interesting scenes, a free people can ever witness. The changes of administration and in every age have most generally been **epochs** of confusion, villainy and bloodshed, in this our happy country take place without any species of distraction, or disorder. This day, has one of the most amiable and worthy men taken that seat to which he is called by the voice of his country. I cannot describe the agitation I felt, while I looked on around on the various multitude and while I listened to an address, containing principles the most correct, sentiments the most **liberal,** and wishes the most **benevolent,** conveyed in the most appropriate and elegant language, and in a manner mild as it was firm. If doubts of the integrity and talents of Mr. Jefferson ever existed in the minds of any one, methinks this address must forever **eradicate** them. The Senate chamber was so crowded that I believe not another creature could enter. On one side of the house the Senate sat, the other was resigned by the representatives to the ladies. . . . It has been conjectured by several gentlemen whom I've asked, that there were near a thousand persons within the walls.

Source: *The Power of Words, Documents in American History: Volume I: To 1877.* New York: HarperCollins College Publishers, 1996.

Primary Source Readings (continued)

DBQ Document-Based Questions

Directions: Use the excerpt to answer the questions below in the spaces provided.

1. **Paraphrasing** According to Margaret Smith, how does America differ in the way power passes from one administration to the next?

_____

_____

2. **Illustrating** How does Smith illustrate the way Jefferson delivered his Inaugural Address?

_____

_____

3. **Explaining** Explain what Smith thinks about the content of Jefferson's speech.

_____

_____

4. **Specifying** Specify the doubts onlookers might have had about Thomas Jefferson.

_____

_____

5. **Making Connections** What are the similarities and differences between Jefferson's inauguration and presidential inaugurations today?

_____

_____

Writing Skills Activity

The Jefferson Era

Writing Poetry

✓ Learning the Skill

Poems can express deep thoughts or paint vivid images in just a few lines. Poets can find inspiration in anything, including nature and historical events. *The Star-Spangled Banner*, for example, is one of the most famous American poems. It was written during the War of 1812. With words, it paints a vivid picture of our flag standing after a battle.

Follow these strategies to learn how to write a poem:

Read Poetry	As you read, pay attention to punctuation marks and the form of *stanzas*, or groups of lines. What type of rhythm do you hear in the poem? Is it fast or slow?
Find Inspiration	There is no limit to what a poem can be written about: plants, animals, climate, people, or places. Consider things in your own life.
Free-Write	Write for 5 to 10 minutes on a topic; write words or phrases that come to mind when you think of that topic.
Sensory Words	Describe images vividly, using the five senses so that the audience can experience what is happening in the poem.
Concrete Images	Images make abstract ideas clear, such as the feeling of happiness. Compare the main theme in your poem to something unrelated, such as comparing life to a walk through a forest.

Poetic Devices	These devices can improve a poem's rhythm and include the following:
	    alliteration—repeated consonant sounds
	    metaphor—comparing two different things
	    rhyme—identical or similar sounds in two or more different words

Draft Your Poem	Choose your words carefully because not all words work well together. Try synonyms or similar sounding words.
Revise and Edit Your Poem	Eliminate unnecessary words or parts of the poem that are not working, such as poor imagery.

Writing Skills Activity (continued)

✔ Practicing the Skill

Directions: Read the poem "The Star-Spangled Banner" by Francis Scott Key, and then answer the questions that follow.

> Oh, say can you see, by the dawn's early light,
> What so proudly we hailed at the twilight's last gleaming?
> Whose broad stripes and bright stars, through the perilous fight,
> O'er the ramparts we watched, were so gallantly streaming?
> And the rocket's red glare, the bombs bursting in air,
> Gave proof through the night that our flag was still there.
> Oh, say does that star-spangled banner yet wave,
> O'er the land of the free and the home of the brave?

1. What was Key's inspiration to write the poem?

_____

2. Which senses does Key trigger in the poem? Give two examples.

_____

_____

3. Name two poetic devices that Key uses, and give examples from the poem.

_____

_____

✔ Applying the Skill

Directions: On a separate sheet of paper, write your own poem describing a time when you waited anxiously for news about an event. First, free-write for 5 to 10 minutes, and do not be concerned about spelling, punctuation, or grammar. Then draft your poem, creating a vivid description. As you write, use poetic devices such as rhyme, metaphor, repetition, and alliteration.

Self-Assessment Checklist

Assess your poem using the checklist below:

- ☐ I described a situation when I anxiously waited for news.
- ☐ I included sensory words.
- ☐ I explained the event using images or symbols.
- ☐ I chose my words carefully.
- ☐ I revised my poem to edit unnecessary words.

Copyright © Glencoe/McGraw-Hill, a division of The McGraw-Hill Companies, Inc.

Chapter

Social Studies Skills Activity

The Jefferson Era

Reading a Flowchart

✔ Learning the Skill

Flowcharts show the steps in a process or a sequence of events. A flowchart could be used to show the movement of goods through a factory or a bill through Congress.

To read a flowchart, follow these steps:

- Read the title or caption of the flowchart to find out what you are studying.
- Read all of the labels or sentences on the flowchart.
- Look for numbers indicating sequence or arrows showing the direction of movement.
- Evaluate the information in the flowchart.

✔ Practicing the Skill

Directions: The flowchart on this page shows a sequence of events that occurred during the 1812 war between the United States and Great Britain. Analyze information in the flowchart, and then answer the questions.

1812 War Between United States and Britain

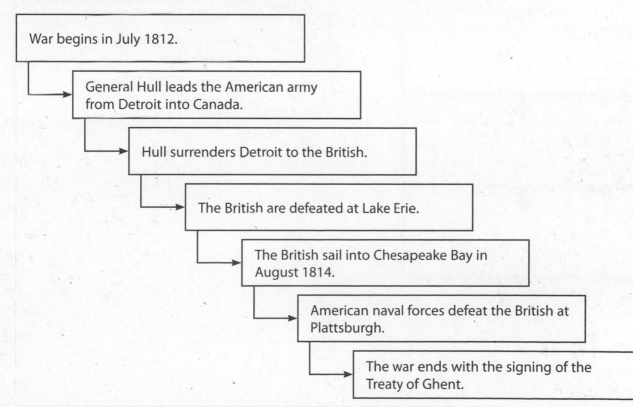

War begins in July 1812.

General Hull leads the American army from Detroit into Canada.

Hull surrenders Detroit to the British.

The British are defeated at Lake Erie.

The British sail into Chesapeake Bay in August 1814.

American naval forces defeat the British at Plattsburgh.

The war ends with the signing of the Treaty of Ghent.

Social Studies Skills Activity (continued)

1. **Describing** What does the flowchart show?

   _____

2. **Relating** How do you know in what sequence the events took place?

   _____

3. **Explaining** What happened after Detroit was surrendered to the British?

   _____

4. **Identifying** What general led the American army into Canada?

   _____

✔ Applying the Skill

Making a Flowchart   DIRECTIONS:
Gather information about the steps
necessary to obtain a public library card, a
photo identification card, or a passport.
Then on a separate sheet of paper, draw a
flowchart similar to the one below. List
the steps in the sequence you should follow. Present your flowchart to the class.

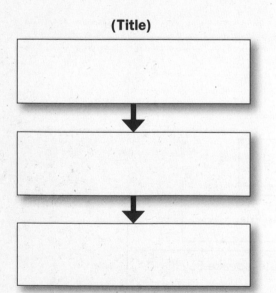

(Title)

Self-Assessment Checklist

Assess your flowchart using the checklist
below:

- ☐ I titled my flowchart.
- ☐ I created a flowchart to show the steps to take to obtain a library card, a photo identification card, or a passport.
- ☐ I made sure the steps were in order and made sense.
- ☐ I explained what I learned about using a flowchart.
- ☐ I presented my flowchart clearly to classmates.

Chapter

Differentiated Instruction Activity

The Jefferson Era

Early Pioneer Medicine

The pioneers who pushed westward beyond the Appalachian Mountains and into the Ohio River valley often relied on remedies such as these when they became sick:

Birch	Tea relieved headaches, kidney stones, and stomach cramps. Poultices helped heal burns, wounds, and bruises.
Borage	Used to relieve depression and reduce fever.
Carrots	A poultice of carrots was applied to boils to draw out the infection.
Catnip	Tea was given to babies with colic or colds.
Cedar	Leaves and twigs of the red cedar were boiled and inhaled for bronchitis.
Cherry	Bark from the wild cherry was used for cough medicine.
Elm	Combined with yeast, crushed elm bark was used as an antiseptic and a poultice for ulcers, especially when there was danger of gangrene.
Feverfew	Used against migraine headache and arthritis.
Ginger	A half teaspoonful in warm water was given to relieve colds or stomach pains.
Horehound	Tea was drunk to relieve the symptoms of a cold and cough.
Onions	Chopped onions were placed in a sick room to prevent spread of contagious diseases.
Peppermint	Tea was given to babies with colic or colds.
Sage	Sage tea was used to relieve an upset stomach. It was also used as a cure for intestinal worms and skin sores.
Sassafras	Tea was used to treat coughs and colds.
Willow	Leaves and bark were made into a tea to break a fever.
White pine	Pitch used to heal wounds and sores. Cooked pine needles used for toothache.
Yarrow	Tea was a remedy for colds. Used in poultices to draw infection out of wounds.

Directions: Use the information from the table and your textbook to answer the following questions on a separate sheet of paper.

1. **Defining** What is a poultice? Which of the items were used to make poultices?

2. **Making Inferences** Why did early pioneers rely on such remedies to cure their ailments?

Differentiated Instruction Activity (continued)

Teaching Strategies for Different Learning Styles

The following activities are ways the basic lesson can be modified to accommodate students' different learning styles.

English Language Learner (ELL)

Have students describe the following ailments from the table in their own words: depression, bronchitis, ulcer, migraine headache, arthritis.

Gifted and Talented

Ask students to use the library or Internet to determine modern medicine's opinion regarding the frontier remedies given in the table. Does science indicate that any of them work? If so, what is the explanation? Students should report their findings in a three- to four-page written report. The report should include flowcharts of two or three remedies and how they changed into today's modern medicine. It should also include visual examples of various ingredients.

Verbal/Linguistic

Ask students to present a five-minute speech about any "home remedies" they are personally acquainted with. Do they (or their families) sometimes try these for minor ailments or aches? Are any similar to the remedies used by the pioneers?

Verbal/Linguistic; Intrapersonal

Ask students to write advertisements of the various frontier remedies as if for an old almanac or catalog (e.g., "Doctor Miracle's Bark of Cherry! Cures Coughs! Colds!" etc.). Provide historical examples or have students find their own online.

Logical/Mathematical

Have students create a chart or table that categorizes the remedies based on the maladies they treat (e.g., all cold remedies in one row, etc.). Encourage them to add other maladies and remedies to the list.

Visual/Spatial

Instruct students to illustrate two or three plants from the table. Illustrations should include a description of what they were used for. Display the drawings in class.

Kinesthetic; Interpersonal

Have students work with a partner to write a dialogue that might have occurred between a frontier healer and a patient suffering from (1) depression, (2) stomach problems, or (3) sore muscles. Students may wish to use the library media center or Internet to find more in-depth information about various remedies. They can then present their dialogues for the class.

Naturalist

Instruct students to provide botanical information about the various plants in the table—where they are found, growing season, scientific names, physical description, and so forth. If feasible, ask students to bring examples of some of the plants to class (purchase at a local nursery, find examples growing in the wild, etc.).

Chapter

Critical Thinking Skills Activity

The Jefferson Era

Analyzing Primary Sources

✓ Learning the Skill

A primary source is a document, such as a letter, newspaper, book, or pamphlet, that was written during a certain period in the past. Historians use primary sources to learn about the past. When you look at a primary source, think about why it was written and who is writing the document to better understand the meaning of the text.

✓ Practicing the Skill

Directions: The excerpt below was written by President Thomas Jefferson to Lewis and Clark prior to their expedition to explore the western lands beyond U.S. territory. Read the excerpt, and then answer the questions that follow on a separate piece of paper.

> The object of your mission is to explore the Missouri River, & such principal streams of it, as, by its course & communication with the waters of the Pacific Ocean . . . may offer the most direct and practicable water communication across the continent for the purposes of commerce. . . . Other objects worthy of notice will be the soil & face of the country, its growth & vegetable productions . . . the animals of the country generally, & especially those not known in the U.S. . . . You will also endeavor to make yourself acquainted . . . with the names of the [Native American] nations and their numbers; the extent & limits of their possession; their relations with other tribes. . . . If a few of their influential chiefs . . . wish to visit with us, arrange such a visit with them, and furnish them with authority to call on our officers.

Source: From a letter from President Thomas Jefferson to Meriwether Lewis and William Clark before their expedition to explore the Louisiana Territory between 1804 and 1806.

1. **Explaining** Why did Jefferson write this letter to Lewis and Clark?

2. **Identifying Central Issues** What seems to be Jefferson's main concern in exploring the new territory? Why would this be a concern?

3. **Analyzing** Does the passage suggest that Jefferson and others in the U.S. government already had some knowledge of the new Louisiana Territory? Explain your answer.

4. **Identifying Points of View** What is Jefferson's attitude toward Native Americans in the letter? Explain your answer.

Critical Thinking Skills Activity (continued)

✓ Applying the Skill

Directions: Use the excerpt to answer the following questions. Circle the letter of the correct answer.

1. Why did Jefferson tell Lewis and Clark to explore the Missouri River?
   A. He wanted to see if it would be a trade link to the Pacific Ocean.
   B. No one had ever seen it before.
   C. It was not included in the Louisiana Purchase.
   D. Jefferson wanted to live on the river.

2. What is the most likely reason that Jefferson wanted Lewis and Clark to report on plant life and soil in the Louisiana Territory?
   A. Jefferson thought Lewis and Clark needed a list of things to keep them busy.
   B. Jefferson wanted to obtain soil from Louisiana to grow his plants.
   C. Jefferson thought the area might not have plant life or soil.
   D. Jefferson wanted to know if the land was fertile and what types of crops might grow there.

3. Which one of the following sources would provide the best firsthand information about Lewis and Clark's journey?
   A. Lewis's letter accepting Jefferson's appointment to make the journey.
   B. Jefferson's memoirs.
   C. Newspaper articles announcing the start of the Lewis and Clark expedition.
   D. Journals kept by the Lewis and Clark expedition.

Geography and History Activity
The Jefferson Era

The Missouri: A Powerful River

River Highways

When traveling across the country today, Americans mostly use highways or airplanes. During the early explorations of our country, however, the transportation systems used most often were rivers. The rivers that carried explorers such as Meriwether Lewis, William Clark, and Zebulon Pike to the West played an important role in their experiences and the development of the young United States.

A Wild Ride

Not long after starting their adventure with the Corps of Discovery, Lewis and Clark realized that surviving the Missouri River would be a major task. The Missouri was a big river—wild and ferocious. While racing downriver, the expedition was assaulted by raging currents, collapsing riverbanks, sandbars, and trees, brush, and vines.

Yet the river's downstream fury was minor compared to the torturous upstream battle. Although Lewis and Clark had sails that could sometimes be used to help the boats struggle upstream, most often the men had to row or use poles to push the boats along. Sometimes they tied ropes to the boats and towed them from the shore, which was grueling work. Navigation was tricky. The men had to crisscross the river to find the safest current, avoid dangerous sandbars, and look out for collapsing riverbanks.

Routes of Some Early Westward Explorers

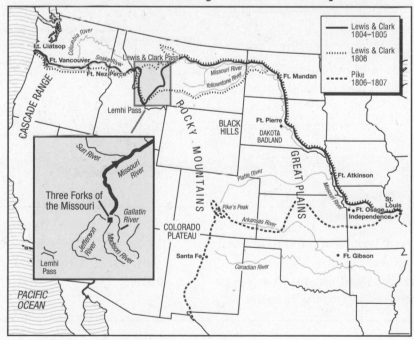

Name_____ Date_____ Class_____

 Geography and History Activity (continued)

A River in Motion

A river on a wide floodplain like the Missouri does not flow in a straight line. Fast-moving channels of deep water, sediments, and objects such as trees in and along the river contribute to the formation of meanders, or curves. The Missouri wound through the landscape in wide-arcing meanders, which greatly affected the Lewis and Clark expedition.

✔ Applying Geography to History

Directions: Use the information in this activity to answer the questions below in the spaces provided.

1. **Making Connections** The Missouri River is nicknamed "Big Muddy." Why do you think the river was given that name?

_____

_____

2. **Summarizing** What difficulties did Lewis and Clark's expedition encounter in navigating the Missouri River?

_____

_____

3. **Identifying** How would curves in the river have affected Lewis and Clark's journey?

_____

_____

4. **Analyzing Visuals** What river did Lewis and Clark navigate on their 1806 journey that they did not navigate on their earlier journey?

_____

_____

5. **Comparing** Looking at the map what do the routes of Lewis and Clark and Zebulon Pike have in common?

_____

_____

_____

GOING FURTHER ▶ ▶▶▶

- Lewis and Clark kept a detailed record of their journey on the Missouri in daily diaries. Read entries from seven consecutive days (on the Internet or in the library). Rewrite the entries in your own words, summarizing the longer entries.

Chapter

Linking Past and Present Activity
The Jefferson Era

Pirates

THEN During the early 1800s, ships in the Mediterranean had to be on guard for pirates from the Barbary Coast states of North Africa. These states included Morocco, Algiers, Tunis, and Tripoli. For years these Barbary pirates terrorized the Mediterranean. They captured ships and took the crews prisoner. If ransom was not paid, the prisoners were enslaved.

To protect their ships from capture, the United States and European governments paid money, or tribute, to the rulers of the Barbary states. After the war between the United States and Tripoli in 1801–1805, Tripoli stopped demanding tribute, but piracy did not end. During the War of 1812, pirates increased their attacks on American ships, and Algiers even declared war on the United States. After an American squadron was sent to Algiers in 1815, Algiers, Tunis, and Tripoli all agreed to stop demanding tribute from the United States.

NOW Today pirates still threaten ships worldwide. Modern pirates armed with knives and guns board vessels. Cargo ships, cruise liners, oil tankers, and even oil rigs are their targets. These attacks have created concern that terrorists may eventually recruit the armed pirates and use their tactics.

Pirates have caused maritime insurance rates to climb. They have stolen cargoes of food, cash and jewelry, and oil shipments. Pirates have kidnapped the crew members of ships and then demanded millions of dollars in ransom.

From 1984 to 2006, more than 4,200 incidents of piracy were reported. The Mediterranean Sea is no longer the main area affected by piracy. Instead, most attacks occur in the South China Sea and the Malacca Strait, the Indian Ocean, East and West Africa, and South America and the Caribbean.

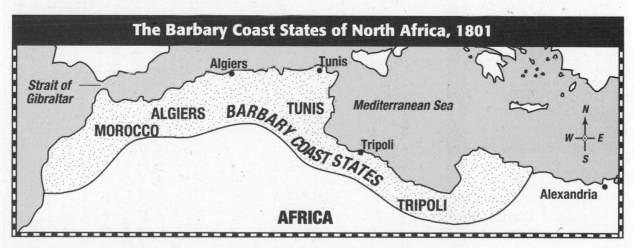

The Barbary Coast States of North Africa, 1801

Comparing and Contrasting DIRECTIONS: Use an atlas or other reference sources to locate a current map of the Barbary Coast region. Compare the region today with the region in the 1800s shown above. What countries occupy the region today? What important cities are located there?

Time Line Activity

The Jefferson Era

Exploring the Louisiana Territory and Other Developments

Directions: Complete the time line by entering the events occurring between 1804 and 1806 in the appropriate spaces

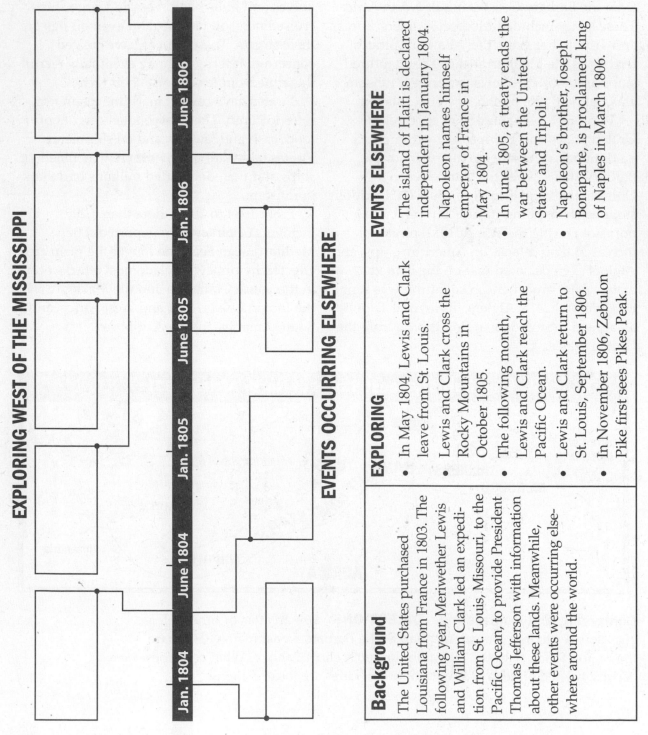

EXPLORING WEST OF THE MISSISSIPPI

Jan. 1804   June 1804   Jan. 1805   June 1805   Jan. 1806   June 1806

EVENTS OCCURRING ELSEWHERE

Background

The United States purchased Louisiana from France in 1803. The following year, Meriwether Lewis and William Clark led an expedition from St. Louis, Missouri, to the Pacific Ocean, to provide President Thomas Jefferson with information about these lands. Meanwhile, other events were occurring elsewhere around the world.

EXPLORING

- In May 1804, Lewis and Clark leave from St. Louis.
- Lewis and Clark cross the Rocky Mountains in October 1805.
- The following month, Lewis and Clark reach the Pacific Ocean.
- Lewis and Clark return to St. Louis, September 1806.
- In November 1806, Zebulon Pike first sees Pikes Peak.

EVENTS ELSEWHERE

- The island of Haiti is declared independent in January 1804.
- Napoleon names himself emperor of France in May 1804.
- In June 1805, a treaty ends the war between the United States and Tripoli.
- Napoleon's brother, Joseph Bonaparte, is proclaimed king of Naples in March 1806.

School-to-Home Connection

The Jefferson Era

What Do You Know?

Directions: Ask each other the following questions to see how much you know about the Jefferson era.*

Student: Why was the Twelfth Amendment passed?

Partner's answer:

Student's answer:

Partner: Why did Napoleon give up his dream of a western empire?

Student: Why did the Embargo Act ban imports from all foreign nations?

Partner's answer:

Student's answer:

Partner: After the War of 1812, who took over the Republican Party?

*With your student, find answers to these questions in the student textbook.

School-to-Home Connection (continued)

Understanding the Essential Questions

Directions: Rewrite each Essential Question as a statement. Then use your textbook to help you write details that support your statement in the graphic organizer provided.

Section 1 In what ways did Thomas Jefferson and the Republicans limit the powers of the government?

Statement: _____

Section 2 How did the Louisiana Purchase affect the nation's economy and politics?

Statement: _____

Ways It Affected the Economy	Ways It Affected Politics

Section 3 What were the challenges to the nation's stability during the late 1700s and early 1800s?

Statement: _____

Threats to Trade	Tensions in the West	War Hawks' Demands

Section 4 How did the United States benefit from its victory in the War of 1812?

Statement: _____

Name_____ Date_____ Class_____

Reteaching Activity
The Jefferson Era

The early 1800s was a time of conflict and change. The Louisiana Purchase doubled the nation's size. Americans pushed westward, resulting in conflicts with Native Americans. In the War of 1812, Americans gained new respect in the world by standing up to the mighty British.

Determining Cause and Effect **DIRECTIONS:** Each phrase listed below describes either a key event of the early 1800s or a factor contributing to an event. Write the phrases in the appropriate boxes in the diagrams.

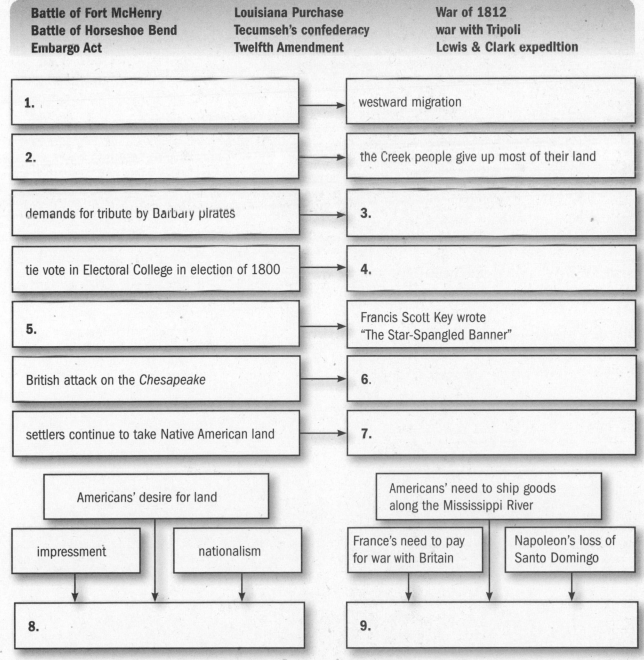

Battle of Fort McHenry	Louisiana Purchase	War of 1812
Battle of Horseshoe Bend	Tecumseh's confederacy	war with Tripoli
Embargo Act	Twelfth Amendment	Lewis & Clark expedition

1. _____ → westward migration

2. _____ → the Creek people give up most of their land

demands for tribute by Barbary pirates → 3. _____

tie vote in Electoral College in election of 1800 → 4. _____

5. _____ → Francis Scott Key wrote "The Star-Spangled Banner"

British attack on the *Chesapeake* → 6. _____

settlers continue to take Native American land → 7. _____

Americans' desire for land

impressment   nationalism

8. _____

Americans' need to ship goods along the Mississippi River

France's need to pay for war with Britain   Napoleon's loss of Santo Domingo

9. _____

Section Resources

Guided Reading Activity

The Jefferson Era

The Republicans Take Power

Reading Tip

As you read the section, take your time and reread sentences that you do not immediately understand. Reading is important for understanding.

Answering Questions   DIRECTIONS: As you read the section, answer the questions below.

1. **Explaining** How did the presidential candidates campaign in 1800?

_____

2. **Determining Cause and Effect** Why did Congress pass the Twelfth Amendment to the Constitution?

_____

3. **Summarizing** What were Jefferson's beliefs concerning the federal government and the states?

_____

_____

4. **Identifying** Which act set up regional courts for the United States?

_____

5. **Analyzing** How did outgoing President Adams ensure Federalist control of the regional courts?

_____

_____

6. **Explaining** What was John Marshall's opinion in *Marbury* v. *Madison*?

_____

_____

7. **Listing** List the three principles of judicial review.

_____

_____

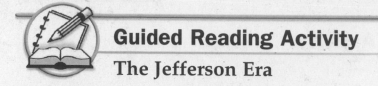

Section

Guided Reading Activity

The Jefferson Era

The Louisiana Purchase

Reading Tip   After reading the section, write down each major heading in the text. Recite the main points of each heading back to a classmate, parent, or teacher without using your text or notes.

Outlining   DIRECTIONS: Reading the section and completing the outline below will help you learn about the Louisiana Purchase.

I. Western Territory

   A. The pioneers' most valued possessions were _____ and

   _____.

   B. In 1800 the area west of the Mississippi River was called the

   _____ _____.

   C. Pioneer farmers shipped their goods downriver to _____.

   D. France's leader, _____, made a secret agreement with Spain to acquire the Louisiana Territory.

   E. Toussaint-Louverture led a successful rebellion in _____.

II. The Nation Expands

   A. Jefferson justified the purchase of Louisiana by the government's

   power to make _____.

   B. An expedition through the newly acquired territory hoped to find and

   map the _____ water route to Asia.

   C. _____ and _____ were chosen to lead the expedition.

   D. The expedition's guide was a Shoshone woman named

   _____.

   E. Expeditions led by _____ traveled through the Great Plains, the Rocky Mountains, and the Rio Grande.

   F. Federalists in Massachusetts plotted to _____ from the Union.

Guided Reading Activity

The Jefferson Era

A Time of Conflict

Reading Tip

Try this note-taking method. Write *who, when, why,* and *what* on a sheet of paper or on separate note cards, and list various phrases under each head as you read the chapter.

Filling in the Blanks   DIRECTIONS: Fill in the blanks using the words in the box and your textbook. Some words may not be used.

Embargo Act	William Henry Harrison	*Chesapeake*
War Hawks	tribute	Prophet
neutral rights	Battle of Tippecanoe	restrictions
Leopard	nationalism	Tripoli
Tecumseh	impressed	Morocco

Barbary Coast pirates demanded **(1)** _____ from governments for the safe passage of ships. When the U.S. government refused to pay more, **(2)** _____ declared war. Once this conflict ended, the United States tried to maintain its **(3)** _____ while Britain and France fought each other. However, Americans became involved when the British navy **(4)** _____ American citizens, and a British warship fired on the American vessel **(5)** _____ .

In retaliation, Congress passed the **(6)** _____ , prohibiting imports from and exports to foreign countries. As a result, American commerce was crippled, and later laws tried to ease trade **(7)** _____ .

Native Americans, led by **(8)** _____ , wanted to ally with the British in Canada to stop American movement westward. Governor **(9)** _____ led forces that defeated the Native Americans at the **(10)** _____ .

Led by Henry Clay and John C. Calhoun, the **(11)** _____ were anxious for war with Britain. Their strong **(12)** _____ appealed to those Americans who wanted to expand the country's territory and power.

Guided Reading Activity

The Jefferson Era

The War of 1812

Reading Tip   Record yourself reading the section out loud. To prepare before class, listen to your audio reading and take notes about it as if it were your teacher lecturing to the entire class.

Reading for Accuracy   **DIRECTIONS:** Use your textbook to decide if a statement is true or false. Write **T** or **F** in the blank. If a statement is false, rewrite it to make it true.

_____ **1.** The United States had a large, well-trained army and state militias when war began.

_____

_____ **2.** American naval forces led by Oliver Hazard Perry defeated the British on Lake Erie.

_____

_____ **3.** The Creeks defeated Andrew Jackson's forces at the Battle of Horseshoe Bend.

_____

_____ **4.** Francis Scott Key wrote "The Star-Spangled Banner" while watching the burning of Washington, D.C.

_____

_____ **5.** After their defeat at the Battle of Lake Champlain, the British decided war with the United States was too costly and unnecessary.

_____

_____ **6.** The Treaty of Ghent addressed the impressment of American sailors.

_____

_____ **7.** The Americans won a decisive victory at the Battle of New Orleans, which occurred after the Treaty of Ghent was signed.

_____

Growth and Expansion

Content Vocabulary Activity

Growth and Expansion

Word Puzzle   DIRECTIONS: The box contains the letters for spelling the terms that match the definitions below. Write the term for each definition and then cross out the letters used to spell it. By the end of question 13, you will have used all but seven letters. Complete question 14 with the extra seven letters.

cotton gin	capital	lock
interchangeable parts	free enterprise	sectionalism
patent	census	state sovereignty
factory system	turnpike	American system
capitalism	canal	

A A A A A A A A A A A A A A A B C C C C C C C C C E E E E E E E E E E E E E E E E E F F G G G H I I I
I I I I I I I I K K L L L L L L L M M M M M N N N N N N N N N N N N O O O O O O P P P P P P R R R R R R
R R R S S S S S S S S S S S S S S S T T T T T T T T T T T T T T T T T T T T U U V Y Y Y Y

1. *Definition:* an efficient process in which all manufacturing steps of a product are brought together in one place

   Term: _____

2. *Definition:* a toll road that is built for easy travel and for the shipment of goods

   Term: _____

3. *Definition:* a person's loyalty to his or her region

   Term: _____

4. *Definition:* an economy where people are free to buy, sell, and produce whatever they want

   Term: _____

5. *Definition:* a simple machine that quickly and efficiently removes seeds from fibers

   Term: _____

6. *Definition:* a program that included a protective tariff, a program of internal improvements, and a national bank

   Term: _____

7. *Definition:* the official count of a population

   Term: _____

8. *Definition:* a document that gives an inventor the sole legal right to an invention and its profits for a certain period of time

   Term: _____

9. *Definition:* an artificial waterway

   Term: _____

10. *Definition:* an economic system where individuals put their money into a business, hoping that the business will be successful and make a profit

   Term: _____

11. *Definition:* a concept that gives states the autonomous power to govern themselves with little interference from national government

   Term: _____

12. *Definition:* identical machine parts that could be put together quickly to make a complete product

   Term: _____

13. *Definition:* a separate compartment where water levels are raised or lowered

   Term: _____

14. *Definition:* money that is invested in a business

   Term: _____

Chapter

Academic Vocabulary Activity
Growth and Expansion

Academic Words in This Chapter

contribute	reveal	intense
element	region	internal

A. Word Meaning Activity: Matching Definitions

Directions: Match the academic words in Column A to their definitions in Column B.

Column A

_____ **1.** contribute

_____ **2.** element

_____ **3.** reveal

_____ **4.** region

_____ **5.** intense

_____ **6.** internal

Column B

A. one of several factors

B. existing in an extreme degree

C. an area with no fixed boundaries

D. relating to the inside of a structure

E. to make known

F. to play a part in bringing about a result

B. Word Meaning Activity: Categorizing Words

Directions: Read the underlined words below, as well as the four words or phrases next to them. Three of the words or phrases are similar in meaning to the underlined word. Circle the word or phrase that is *not similar* to the under-lined word.

1. contribute: help, inhibit, participate, assist

2. element: ingredient, component, aspect, sum

3. reveal: conceal, disclose, unmask, discover

4. region: district, territory, map, zone

5. intense: fierce, profound, moderate, forceful

6. internal: inner, exterior, interior, central

Academic Vocabulary Activity (continued)

C. Word Family Activity: Identifying Parts of Speech

Directions: A *noun* is a word that names a person, a place, a thing, or an idea. A *verb* is a word that is used to describe an action, an experience, or a state of being. An *adjective* is a word used to describe a noun. Determine whether the words below are in noun, verb, or adjective form. Put a check mark (√) in the appropriate column. Some words have more than one form.

Words	Noun	Verb	Adjective
1. contribute			
2. contribution			
3. contributing			
4. element			
5. elemental			
6. revealed			
7. revealing			
8. revelation			
9. region			
10. regional			
11. intense			
12. intenseness			
13. internal			

Chapter

Primary Source Reading Activity

Growth and Expansion

Why We Need a Protective Tariff

Interpreting the Source

Before the War of 1812, the United States was dependent on other countries, especially Great Britain, for manufactured goods. The war cut off the supply of British goods and helped stimulate American manufacturing. After the war, when the British again began offering inexpensive manufactured goods, the new American companies cried out for protection against European competition. The following newspaper editorial from the *Niles Weekly Register* supports a protective tariff and predicts what will happen to American factories without such protection.

Guided Reading

As you read, identify ways in which each group of people in the community benefited from the Waltham factory's presence.

Reader's Dictionary

manufactory: factory

eminence: hill

tariff: a charge placed on imported goods

industrious: hard-working

frugal: avoiding waste

The Waltham [Massachusetts] **manufactory** is the largest and probably the most prosperous in the United States. . . . When foreign . . . writers tell us, your country is not fit for manufactures, we can with pride tell them—look at Waltham. . . .

It would give me much pleasure to seat myself on an **eminence** near Waltham with some honest anti-**tariffite** and for one day watch the motions of all the in-comers and out-goers at the village and factory; to take a note of what they brought in and took out; to ask the passing farmer what he took to market, the price he obtained, and what he brought home in exchange; to ask the fond mother who had been to see her children whether their habits were **industrious, frugal,** moral, and how much of their earnings went to the comforts of their aged parents. I would ask one of the worthy mercantile proprietors what effect it had on his commercial pursuits. And I would cheerfully agree to give up all my tariff doctrines if the answers of all would not be as I could wish.

If my anti-tariff friend would not be convinced, I would put him this case. Suppose this fine factory should be destroyed by fire and the proprietors should not rebuild it. We will suppose ourselves sitting on this same hill one year after the [factory was] in ruins, and the same farmer, the same mother, and the same merchant should all join us, and we should join in the conversation, comparing the past with the present, the farmer's market, the mother's children, the merchant's business.

Primary Source Reading Activity (continued)

> Every man of this description ought to go to Waltham, or some other manufactory, and imagine to himself the difference between a factory at work and a factory burnt. This is the mode of settling questions of political economy and national policy. . . . When [people] see the practical difference between a factory stopped and a factory active, the nation will cease to be divided and Congress indifferent.

Source: *Niles Weekly Register;* June 23, 1821.

DBQ Document-Based Questions

Directions: Answer the questions in the spaces provided.

1. **Illustrating** In what ways does the author illustrate how a protective tariff will benefit people in his town?

_____

_____

2. **Speculating** How would the entire town be affected if the factory were to close?

_____

_____

3. **Synthesizing** According to the editorial, what is the proper method for settling questions of economic and national policy?

_____

_____

4. **Making Connections** Why might an autoworker employed by an American manufacturer favor a protective tariff today? Why might American consumers oppose such a tariff?

_____

_____

_____

Writing Skills Activity
Growth and Expansion

Writing "Business" Documents

✓ Learning the Skill

Clearly presenting information helps the writer and the reader understand each other and avoid confusion. Accurately presenting information in a business document such as a job description, for example, will help keep the employer and the potential employee from being disappointed. You might want to offer your services as a babysitter by posting a notice on a bulletin board at your grocery store. What information will you need to convey to potential customers?

Business documents must give the information the intended audience needs and must do so quickly. A potential customer for your babysitting services would want to know if you have experience, when you are available, what you expect to be paid, and how to contact you. Your poster might read: "Babysitter with 3 years' experience available weekends, $5/hour. Contact [your name] at 555-1234."

Follow these steps to write a good job description:

• Identify the duties required for this job.

• Identify the skills that are needed to perform those duties.

• Identify other relevant information for the job (location, hours, salary, etc.).

• Write your job description. Remember to present the information concisely.

✓ Practicing the Skill

Directions: Read the job posting below, and then answer the following questions.

(a) Blacksmith available at 17 Orchard Lane. (b) Skilled in making and repairing farming implements and household items. (c) Also skilled in designing decorative wrought iron pieces. (d) Tall male with excellent dancing skills. (e) Reasonable rates.

---

1. Which sentence tells you what type of job this person performs? Why?

_____

_____

_____

Writing Skills Activity (continued)

2. Which sentence(s) describes what this person can do relating to the job?

_____

_____

3. Which sentence does not belong? Why?

_____

_____

_____

✔ Applying the Skill

Directions: Imagine that you are Francis Cabot Lowell, owner of a textile manufacturing company, and you are looking for someone to manage one of your factories. Write a help wanted ad for this job. Be sure to list the job responsibilities, as well as the experience and skills that this person should have. Include other relevant information as desired.

_____

_____

_____

_____

_____

_____

_____

_____

_____

_____

_____

_____

Self-Assessment Checklist

Assess your help wanted ad using the checklist below:

☐ I identified duties to be performed.

☐ I identified skills and experience required for the job.

☐ I provided all relevant information.

☐ I presented information concisely.

Chapter

Social Studies Skills Activity

Growth and Expansion

Creating a Web Diagram

✓ Learning the Skill

Web diagrams are used to help you identify one central idea and organize related information around it. They allow you to identify ideas related to secondary information.

To create a web diagram, use the following steps:

- Place the central idea for your web diagram in the center circle.
- Determine the broad categories that should be listed in the outer ovals or circles of the web diagram and enter the information in the ovals or circles.
- Add relevant, factual material to help explain or illustrate the broad categories.

✓ Practicing the Skill

Organizing   DIRECTIONS: As the United States grew, advances in transportation aided in its economic growth and expansion. Complete the web diagram below by adding one detail about each form of transportation.

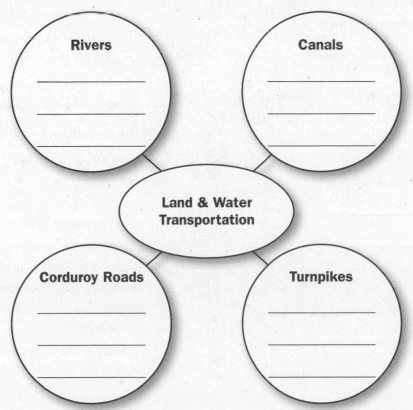

Social Studies Skills Activity (continued)

✓ Applying the Skill

Organizing **DIRECTIONS:** Following the War of 1812, Americans' sense of national unity grew. This nationalism helped shape U.S. foreign policy. On a separate sheet of paper, create your own web diagram similar to the one below. In it show details about U.S. foreign affairs after the War of 1812. Be sure to add one detail about each agreement or policy in your web.

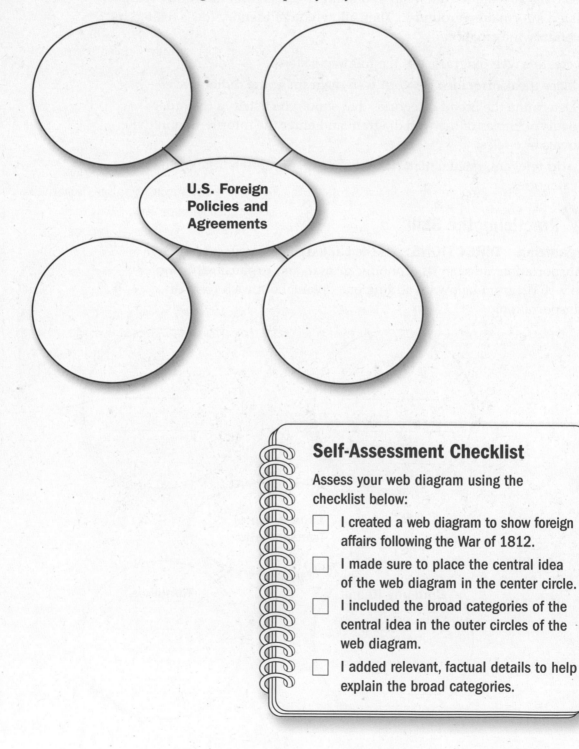

U.S. Foreign Policies and Agreements

Self-Assessment Checklist

Assess your web diagram using the checklist below:

☐ I created a web diagram to show foreign affairs following the War of 1812.

☐ I made sure to place the central idea of the web diagram in the center circle.

☐ I included the broad categories of the central idea in the outer circles of the web diagram.

☐ I added relevant, factual details to help explain the broad categories.

Differentiated Instruction Activity
Growth and Expansion

The Monroe Doctrine

Read the following excerpt from James Monroe's speech to Congress on December 2, 1823. Then answer the questions that follow.

> [T]he occasion has been judged proper for asserting, as a principle in which the rights and interests of the United States are involved, that the American continents, by the free and independent condition which they have assumed and maintain, are henceforth not to be considered as subjects for future colonization by any European power. . . .
>
> . . . The citizens of the United States cherish sentiments the most friendly in favor of the liberty and happiness of their fellow-men on that side of the Atlantic. In the wars of the European powers in matters relating to themselves we have never taken any part, nor does it comport with our policy so to do. It is only when our rights are invaded or seriously menaced that we resent injuries or make preparations for our defense. With the movements in this hemisphere we are of necessity more immediately connected, and by causes which must be obvious to all enlightened and impartial observers. . . . We owe it, therefore, to candor and to the amicable relations existing between the United States and those [European] powers to declare that we should consider any attempt on their part to extend their system to any portion of this hemisphere as dangerous to our peace and safety. With the existing colonies or dependencies of any European power we have not interfered and shall not interfere. But with the [Latin American] governments who have declared their independence and maintain it, and whose independence we have, on great consideration and on just principles, acknowledged, we could not view any interposition for the purpose of oppressing them or controlling in any other manner their destiny by any European power in any other light than as the manifestation of an unfriendly disposition toward the United States. . . .

Directions: Use the information from the speech excerpt and your textbook to answer the following questions on a separate sheet of paper.

1. **Finding the Main Idea** What are the main points of the excerpts?

2. **Contrasting** What distinctions does Monroe make between European colonies and independent Latin American nations?

Differentiated Instruction Activity (continued)

Teaching Strategies for Different Learning Styles

The following activities are ways the basic lesson can be modified to accommodate students' different learning styles.

English Language Learner (ELL)

The "Read and Say Something" strategy helps students with reading comprehension—especially for difficult reading material. Have students read the first four lines of the excerpt, then turn to a partner and say something about the reading. Tell students they should say anything they want related to the selection, such as their reactions to ideas, descriptions, or anything they find confusing. Solicit information from the entire class about what each pair discussed.

Gifted and Talented

At the time of Monroe's speech, the United States did not have the military or economic power to enforce his ideas. What if, realizing this, Monroe had decided *against* issuing his doctrine? What might have been the effect on (1) America's relationship with Europe, especially Great Britain; (2) America's relationship with Latin America, (3) westward expansion of the United States, and (4) the future of America as a "world player"? Ask students to speculate on this in a four-page paper.

Verbal/Linguistic; Intrapersonal

Ask students to assume the role of the foreign minister of Spain and write a two-page response to Monroe's speech.

Logical/Mathematical

Have students create a time line showing the dates of independence of Latin American countries within 20 years before and 20 years after Monroe's speech. Students should write two or three paragraphs speculating about the impact of Monroe's speech on their findings.

Visual/Spatial

Ask students to draw an editorial cartoon explaining the Monroe Doctrine and expressing their opinions about it.

Auditory/Musical

Following the War of 1812, Americans felt a new sense of pride in their country. Ask students to bring to class an example of a song that was popular with Americans in the first two decades of the 1800s (either a recording or sheet music and lyrics). As students listen to/read the selections, lead the class in a discussion about any nationalistic elements they may contain. You will need to provide a CD/tape player for this activity.

Kinesthetic; Interpersonal

Organize the class into two or three groups, and instruct each to work together to create a board game called The Monroe Doctrine. (Consider providing students with examples of several "world politics" games such as Risk to stimulate ideas.) Students should base their games on historical realities of the early 1800s, but otherwise should be allowed to design the games however they choose—including how the game is won. They should create their own game pieces, cards, maps, and all other items needed to play the game. Allow each group to demonstrate their game in class.

Below Grade Level

Have students examine the excerpts and read about the Monroe Doctrine in their textbook. Then have them write six questions that they might ask about the material. Students should use a different question starter for each question: *who, what, when, where, why,* and *how.*

Critical Thinking Skills Activity

Growth and Expansion

Analyzing Information

✓ Learning the Skill

Analyzing information involves breaking it into meaningful parts so that it can be understood, allowing you to form an opinion about it. The ability to analyze information helps you establish positions on issues that can affect your life. For example, you need to analyze a candidate's statements to determine whether or not to vote for the candidate.

Use the following guidelines to help you analyze information:

• Identify the topic that is being discussed.

• Examine how the information is organized, and determine the main points.

• Summarize the information in your own words, and then form an opinion about it based on your understanding of the topic.

✓ Practicing the Skill

Directions: The excerpt below is from President James Monroe's speech to Congress on December 2, 1823. Read the excerpt, and answer the questions that follow.

> We owe it, therefore, to candor and to the amicable [friendly] relations existing between the United States and those [European] powers to declare that we should consider any attempt on their part to extend their system to any portion of this hemisphere as dangerous to our peace and safety. With the existing colonies or dependencies of any European power we have not interfered and shall not interfere. But with the governments who have declared their independence and maintain it, and whose independence we have, on great consideration and on just principles, acknowledged, we could not view any interposition [interference] for the purpose of oppressing them or controlling in any other manner their destiny by any European power in any other light than as the manifestation of an unfriendly disposition toward the United States.

Source: The Monroe Doctrine http://www.britannica.com/eb/article-9116944/Document_James_Monroe_The_Monroe_ Doctrine Preferred by Britannica: http://www.britannica.com/eb/article-9053434

1. **Naming** What is the subject of the excerpt?

_____

_____

Critical Thinking Skills Activity (continued)

2. Identifying Central Issues What are the main points in the excerpt?

_____

_____

3. Describing How would you describe the organization of the excerpt?

_____

_____

✓ Applying the Skill

Directions: Use the information in the excerpt to answer the following questions. Circle the letter of the correct answer.

1. What might James Monroe view as an objectionable European influence?
   A. a city with a European cultural influence
   B. a European country controlling a major port city in North America
   C. the United States recognizing a religious holiday that originated in Europe
   D. the United States importing goods from Europe

2. Which of the following would President Monroe most likely support?
   A. imposing the laws of the United States on European colonies in North America
   B. aiding a European colony in acquiring its freedom from Europe
   C. incorporating a European colony's laws into the federal laws of the United States
   D. fighting to stop European interference in the Western Hemisphere

3. Which of the following would President Monroe most likely oppose?
   A. trading with European countries
   B. U.S. interference with existing European colonies
   C. European immigrants living in the United States
   D. westward expansion

Chapter

Geography and History Activity
Growth and Expansion

Changing Boundaries of the United States

In the years following the War of 1812, many Americans realized that if the United States were to prosper, it needed good relations with European powers. At the same time, the United States had a growing desire to settle its borders and to claim more territory as its own.

The Northern Boundary

Following the Revolutionary War, British-owned Canada and the United States settled on a boundary line from Lake of the Woods to the East coast. Americans pushed to extend the border westward, primarily to gain access to the Pacific Ocean. At the Convention of 1818, Britain agreed to extend the American-Canadian boundary at the 49th parallel. However, the British resisted giving up Oregon Country. The conflict over Oregon almost led to war, but a peaceful settlement was reached. Britain and the United States agreed to share the territory. The number of Americans settling the Oregon territory far outnumbered the British and in 1846 the British agreed to extend the border all the way to the Pacific Coast.

The Southwestern Boundary

By 1821, Mexico was free from Spain and gained control of the land from present-day Texas to the Pacific Ocean. Hoping it would help them economically, the Mexicans offered large land grants to attract American settlers into Texas. Many Americans accepted the offer. However, disputes over land ownership and cultural differences eventually resulted in the Texas settlers fighting for independence from Mexico.

The Texas Revolution lasted only a few months, and in 1836 Texas became an independent republic. In 1845 the Republic of Texas became the 28th state. However, the Mexican government disputed the southern border of Texas. That same year, still eager for westward expansion, the United States offered to purchase the Mexican territories of California and New Mexico. Some Mexicans were offended. The conflict broke into war in 1846. In 1848 Mexico agreed to sign a peace treaty that extended the United States all the way to the Pacific.

Western United States in 1824

Geography and History Activity (continued)

Applying Geography to History

Directions: Using the information on the previous page answer the following questions in the spaces provided.

1. **Applying** In 1818 the British agreed to extend the northern border of the United States to the edge of Oregon Country from what location?

   _____

2. **Stating** What geographic advantage did the United States seek to gain by owning the Oregon Country?

   _____

   _____

3. **Locating** In 1824 what were the two most western American states?

   _____

4. **Analyzing** From a defense standpoint, how did gaining the Mexican territories from Texas to the Pacific Ocean affect America's security?

   _____

   _____

5. **Comparing and Contrasting** In 1846 what was the major difference in how the United States resolved border disputes with Britain and Mexico?

   _____

   _____

GOING FURTHER ▶ ▶▶▶

- The war with Mexico (1846–1848) was fought over boundary disputes with the United States. The map and legend show the areas belonging to the U.S., Britain, and Mexico in 1824. Create a second map and legend indicating the areas held by each country after the war ended.

Linking Past and Present Activity
Growth and Expansion

Refrigeration

THEN In the 1820s, Americans used ice for refrigeration. Frederick Tudor designed a new kind of saw to cut ice from ponds. Tudor cut the ice into blocks of the same size and shape, so it packed into carts and shipped more easily. Soon Nathaniel Jarvis Wyeth discovered that sawdust prevented ice from melting in transit. By the 1830s, Tudor cut 1,000 tons (907 t) of ice each day in Massachusetts and shipped it to distant countries such as Persia and India.

Tudor also designed a more efficient ice-storage house, which reduced the seasonal loss of ice in hot climates. His technique led to the invention of the icebox, a miniature ice-storage house for the kitchen. Tudor encouraged ice cream and iced drink consumption, and iceboxes quickly became a middle-class necessity.

Refrigeration System

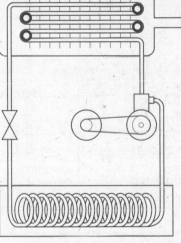

NOW Today we take refrigeration for granted. The most widely used system is the vapor compression system. (See the diagram.) A refrigerant (a vapor that melts and freezes at a low temperature) boils at a temperature low enough to absorb heat from the space being cooled. A compressor removes the vapor at a rate that keeps the pressure and temperature in the evaporator low. The compressor sends the refrigerant to a condenser. The condenser distributes heat to circulating water or air and returns the condensed refrigerant to the evaporator for another cycle.

Conducting an Experiment
DIRECTIONS: On a separate sheet of paper, complete the lab activity report. Use three ice cubes of the same size. Measure how long it takes an ice cube to melt in: (1) an airtight plastic bowl, (2) a sock, and (3) a container in which dirt is packed around the ice. How does this experiment help you understand Wyeth and Tudor's accomplishments?

ACTIVITY REPORT

Data Collection

1. **Airtight plastic bowl**

    Melting Time: _____ minutes _____ seconds

2. **Sock**

    Melting Time: _____ minutes _____ seconds

3. **Dirt packed around ice in a container**

    Melting Time: _____ minutes _____ seconds

Data Comparison

1. Which cube melted fastest?
2. Which cube melted slowest?

Conclusions

Chapter

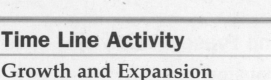

Time Line Activity

Growth and Expansion

Technology: Textiles and Transportation (1790–1825)

Directions: Use your textbook and the information in the time line to answer the questions in the spaces provided.

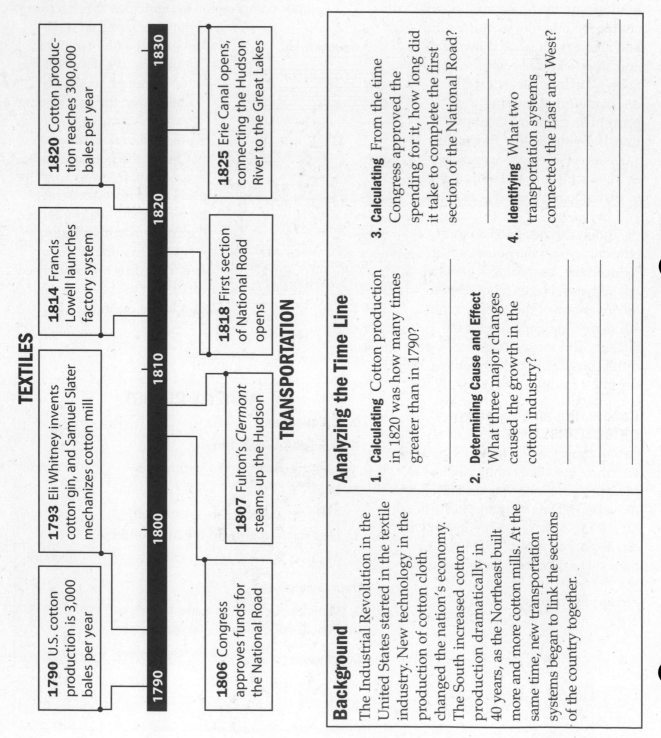

TEXTILES

1790 U.S. cotton production is 3,000 bales per year

1793 Eli Whitney invents cotton gin, and Samuel Slater mechanizes cotton mill

1814 Francis Lowell launches factory system

1820 Cotton production reaches 300,000 bales per year

TRANSPORTATION

1806 Congress approves funds for the National Road

1807 Fulton's *Clermont* steams up the Hudson

1818 First section of National Road opens

1825 Erie Canal opens, connecting the Hudson River to the Great Lakes

Background

The Industrial Revolution in the United States started in the textile industry. New technology in the production of cotton cloth changed the nation's economy. The South increased cotton production dramatically in 40 years, as the Northeast built more and more cotton mills. At the same time, new transportation systems began to link the sections of the country together.

Analyzing the Time Line

1. **Calculating** Cotton production in 1820 was how many times greater than in 1790?

2. **Determining Cause and Effect** What three major changes caused the growth in the cotton industry?

3. **Calculating** From the time Congress approved the spending for it, how long did it take to complete the first section of the National Road?

4. **Identifying** What two transportation systems connected the East and West?

Chapter

School-to-Home Connection
Growth and Expansion

What Do You Know?

Directions: Ask each other the following questions to see how much you know about the economic and physical growth of the United States in the early 1800s.*

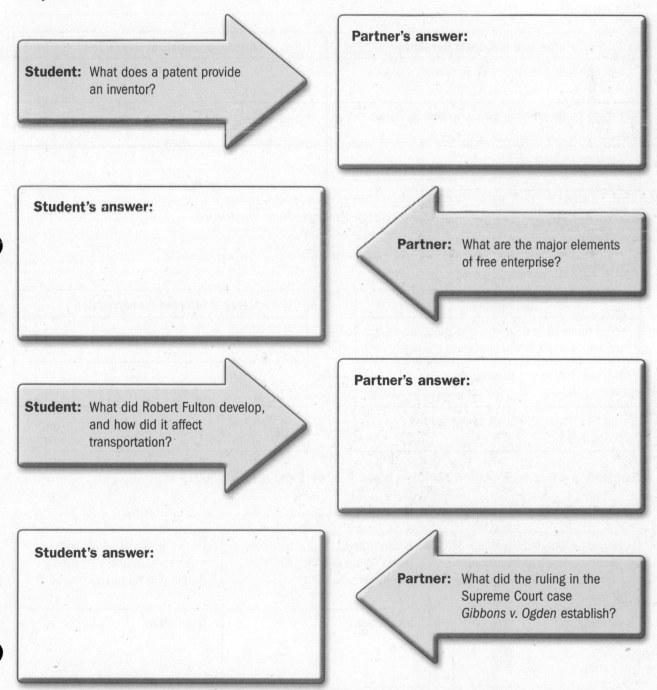

Student: What does a patent provide an inventor?

Partner's answer:

Student's answer:

Partner: What are the major elements of free enterprise?

Student: What did Robert Fulton develop, and how did it affect transportation?

Partner's answer:

Student's answer:

Partner: What did the ruling in the Supreme Court case *Gibbons v. Ogden* establish?

*With your student, find answers to these questions in the student textbook.

Name_____ Date_____ Class_____

 School-to-Home Connection (continued)

Understanding the Essential Questions

Directions: Rewrite each Essential Question as a statement. Then use your textbook to help you write details that support your statement in the graphic organizer provided.

Section 1 What effects did the Industrial Revolution have on the U.S. economy?

Statement: _____

Before the Industrial Revolution	After the Industrial Revolution
Most people worked in homes or workshops.	
People made the things they needed by hand.	
Businesses were small.	

Section 2 How did land and water transportation affect westward expansion?

Statement: _____

Improvement		How It Affected Transportation
More roads were built and improved, including toll roads and a national road to the West.	⇨	
The steamboat was developed.	⇨	
The Erie Canal and other canals were constructed.	⇨	

Section 3 How were nation-building issues resolved in the early 1800s?

Statement: _____

Issue: Sectional differences became more intense because of the issue of allowing slavery in new states.	**Issue:** Conflicts arose between states' rights and the federal government.	**Issue:** Territorial issues with European nations, particularly Britain and Spain, developed.
Resolution:	**Resolution:**	**Resolution:**

Reteaching Activity

Growth and Expansion

From 1795 to 1825, the United States grew as a nation. Around 1800, the Industrial Revolution began to take root in the United States. The economy expanded as new technologies simplified work and improvements in transportation linked different parts of the country. Political disputes within the country and with other nations were settled. Prosperity and peace came together to create an "Era of Good Feelings."

Identifying **DIRECTIONS:** The phrases below identify new technologies and agreements that helped the nation grow and prosper. Write each phrase next to its contribution in the chart.

Adams-Onís Treaty	Monroe Doctrine	Missouri Compromise
canals	cotton gin	patents
capitalism	factory system	Rush-Bagot Treaty
Clermont	interchangeable parts	turnpikes

Technologies and Agreements	Contributions
1.	expanded the United States by adding Florida
2.	increased efficiency by bringing all manufacturing steps together in one place
3.	temporarily settled the issue of slavery in new states
4.	made cotton production more efficient
5.	system of toll roads that made the shipment of goods easier
6.	provided for disarmament along the Great Lakes border with Canada
7.	encouraged invention by protecting inventors' rights
8.	helped bring about a new age of steam-powered river travel
9.	economic system that allows individuals to invest in businesses
10.	allowed large-scale production of goods and lower prices
11.	warned that the United States would not tolerate any more European colonization in North or South America
12.	provided a water transportation link between the East and West

Section Resources

Guided Reading Activity
Growth and Expansion

Economic Growth

Reading Tip Give yourself enough time to read and understand the text. Don't rush through it. Take your time and pause to reread sections or to think about what you have just read.

Answering Questions DIRECTIONS: As you read the section, answer the questions below.

1. **Analyzing** How did geography contribute to the Industrial Revolution in New England?

_____

_____

2. **Summarizing** What were the advantages of using interchangeable parts?

_____

_____

3. **Defining** What is a patent?

_____

4. **Explaining** What is the factory system?

_____

5. **Naming** Name two terms that describe the economy of the United States.

_____

6. **Listing** What are the major elements of free enterprise?

_____

7. **Determining Cause and Effect** Why did shopkeepers, merchants, and farmers invest in new businesses?

_____

_____

8. **Analyzing** Why did many cities develop along waterways?

_____

_____

Guided Reading Activity

Growth and Expansion

Westward Bound

Reading Tip As you read the section, write down the five most important points of the reading. Review your list against the text to make any revisions. Then summarize each point to use as a study guide.

Outlining   DIRECTIONS: As you read the section complete the outline below.

I. Moving West

   A. The first _____ in 1790 determined that the nation had a population of almost 4 million people.

   B. Travelers paid fees to travel on toll roads called _____.

   C. Congress approved the building of a(n) _____ to the West.

   D. River travel westward was not easy because most rivers in the eastern region flowed _____ to _____.

   E. The problem of traveling upstream against a current was addressed by _____ with powerful engines.

II. Canals

   A. _____ led officials in developing the plan to link New York City with the Great Lakes.

   B. The _____ connected Albany and Buffalo.

   C. Boats were raised and lowered in canals by means of _____.

III. Western Settlement

   A. Waves in the movement westward resulted in the admission of new _____ to the nation.

   B. Pioneers typically settled in communities along major _____.

Section

Guided Reading Activity

Growth and Expansion

Guided R...
Growth an...
Bound

Unity and Sectionalism

Reading Tip If you come across a complicated paragraph, try reading it aloud. Read carefully and clearly, and pause to separate complete thoughts. Reread it if necessary.

Filling in the Blanks   **DIRECTIONS:** Use your textbook to fill in the blanks using the words in the box. Some words may not be used.

John C. Calhoun	American System	Adams-Onís
external	Daniel Webster	Mexico
Canada	Good Feelings	sovereignty
Henry Clay	Monroe Doctrine	Rush-Bagot
sectionalism	Missouri Compromise	internal

The spread of national unity after the War of 1812 was called the Era of **(1)** _____.

However, regional loyalty, or **(2)** _____, increased debate over national policies

concerning slavery, tariffs, and **(3)** _____ improvements.

(4) _____ of South Carolina championed the concept of state

(5) _____. New England's **(6)** _____ supported policies that would

strengthen the North and the nation. Although **(7)** _____ represented Western

interests, he also tried to resolve sectional differences with his program of policies called the

(8) _____. However, he was more successful in his efforts with the

(9) _____, which preserved the balance between North and South on the

slavery issue.

Foreign relations with Britain and Spain involved boundaries and treaties. The boundary

with **(10)** _____ was set at the 49th parallel. The United States gave up its claims to

Spanish Texas in the **(11)** _____ Treaty. The **(12)** _____ essentially

closed North and South America to future colonization by European nations.

Answer Key

Launching the Republic

Citizenship and Decision-Making Activity

Questions to Consider

1. Answers will vary, but they should reflect an understanding of the impact of the right. For example, students might recognize freedom of religion as impacting their right to attend a church of their choice.

2. Answers will vary, but students should recognize that the rights expressed in the Bill of Rights impact them regularly.

3. Answers will vary, but students should be able to describe how the Bill of Rights affects their daily lives.

Your Task

Check students' Self-Assessment Checklists. Students should complete the Citizenship and Decision-Making Activity by working in a group as directed in the How to Do It section. At the end of the project, have students review their work by discussing difficulties they may have faced during the project and how they resolved those difficulties. Encourage students to explain how they would improve their work if they did this project again.

Economics and History Activity

Applying Economics to History

1. Students should identify three main points: Government should pass laws to prevent people from harming one another. Other than that activity, government should not interfere in business or in people's lives. Government should not take away people's earnings by taxing them.

2. Jefferson would oppose an income tax. He said that government "shall not take from labor the bread it has earned." He is using "bread" to stand for income, so he is saying that government should not take income away from workers. In other words, it should not tax their income.

3. Laissez-faire holds that government should not interfere with the economy.

4. Government passes laws to maintain fair competition and protect consumers from harm, provides goods and services that benefit society as a whole, and runs programs to help elderly people and those living in poverty.

5. In 2006 the federal government spent the largest portion of its money on the Social Security program.

6. The government spent $2,655 billion x 0.085 = $226 billion in interest on the national debt.

Going Further With Economics

Answers will vary depending on students' values and points of view. Students should create circle graphs that show how they think the federal government should spend its money and should provide an explanation for the percentages on their graphs. All of the percentages on the graphs should total 100.

Reading Skills Activity

Practicing the Skill

Details may include: river travel was more convenient than overland travel; east-west and upstream river travel was difficult; early steam engines could not overcome problems associated with river travel; Fulton's steamboat, the *Clermont*, made river travel much faster than ever before.

Students' summaries may be similar to the following: Though river travel was superior to overland travel in early America, it could still be difficult to transport people and goods exactly where they wanted to go. Steamboats greatly improved the flow of people and goods along rivers.

Applying the Skill

Details may include: existing river system prevented steamboats from connecting eastern and western United States; business leaders developed a plan to build an east-west canal;

Answer Key

the Erie Canal successfully linked Albany, New York, with Buffalo, New York; additional canals built after the triumph of the Erie Canal made travel easier and cheaper, which united the country.

Students' summaries may be similar to the following: Business and government officials helped develop a system of canals to link the eastern and western parts of the country. Canals made travel easier and helped make America a prosperous, unified country.

American Literature Reading

1. At that time, no paths existed at all. Since then, narrow roads had been cleared. On Marmaduke's first exploration there were no mills, roads, towns, or farms. Since then, farms had sprung up and now produced plenty of food.

2. because they had not yet cleared land for farming

3. Marmaduke himself explored the area in search of profit; other adventurers, he said, were induced by widespread hardships to seek adventure and settle in unexplored territory.

Interpreting Political Cartoons

1. The turtle represents the Embargo Act.

2. The man with the barrel is a smuggler trying to smuggle cargo to the waiting ship.

3. The Union Jack on the ship's stern tells us it is British. It is waiting to take on the smuggled cargo.

4. The key to the meaning is understanding that *ograbme* is *embargo* spelled backwards. The word refers to the Embargo Act, and the pun is that the turtle (the Act) is grabbing the smuggler in its mouth.

5. The cartoonist is in favor of the act. The evidence is that the smuggler is drawn unfavorably, while the other man is not.

6. Answers will vary. Some possibilities: "Bar me," "O bar me," "mob rage," and "Go rob me."

7. The effectiveness of the Embargo Act is questionable, because it stirred up domestic ferment and hurt the United States Further, the United States ultimately was not able to maintain its neutrality. Answers will vary. Make sure answers are supported by facts and reasons.

The Federalist Era

Content Vocabulary Activity

1. partisan
2. cabinet
3. neutrality
4. caucus
5. bond
6. alien
7. unconstitutional
8. impressment
9. states rights
10. precedent
11. nullify
12. national debt
13. sedition
14. implied powers
15. tariff

Academic Vocabulary Activity

A. Word Meaning
1. S   3. S   5. A
2. A   4. S   6. A

B. Word Usage
1. challenge   4. maintain
2. principle   5. resolve
3. uniform   6. accumulate

C. Word Usage
1. e   4. a
2. d   5. c
3. b

Primary Source Readings

1. The "five freedoms" are freedom of religion, freedom of speech, freedom of the press, freedom to assemble peaceably, and freedom to petition the government to deal with their complaints.

Answer Key

2. Responses will vary. This Amendment is open to wide interpretation. Essentially, it grants people the right to own weapons and to form state-sponsored militias, such as the National Guard.

3. The police must obtain a court-ordered search warrant to search a person's house, car, or other personal property. The police must show "probable cause" before they can arrest a person.

4. A person accused of a crime must have a speedy, public trial by an impartial jury in the place where the crime occurred. He or she must understand the charges, be permitted to confront the witnesses during the trial, be able to provide his or her own witnesses, and have an attorney to defend the case.

5. Amendment IX and Amendment X reserve the rights in general to the states and to the people.

Writing Skills Activity

Practicing the Skill

Federalists: emphasis on manufacturing, British alliance, protective taxes, Alexander Hamilton

Democratic Republicans: strong state governments, strict interpretation of the Constitution, state banks, Thomas Jefferson

Applying the Skill

Check students' Self-Assessment Checklist.
1. Legislation: Alien and Sedition Acts

Why it was necessary: to protect nation's security from aliens living in the United States if the United States went to war with France

What did it say: allowed the president to imprison aliens or send those considered dangerous out of the country
2. Virginia and Kentucky Resolutions

Why it was necessary: to protest strong central government

What did it say: states may nullify federal laws considered unconstitutional; federal government should be limited to the powers clearly assigned by the Constitution

Social Studies Skills Activity

Practicing the Skill
1. The source of the speech is Alexander Hamilton's speech at the Constitutional Convention of 1787.

2. The main topic of the speech stresses the strong, centralized national government by a few.

3. Students' answers will vary. Hamilton's message is that the people cannot be trusted to make clear decisions. Some students might say that Hamilton distrusted democracy.

Applying the Skill

Students' Venn diagrams and summaries will vary but should include some of the following main points.

Similarities:

Both statesmen agree that there will be a continuing community of U.S. citizens, and they are working toward that end.

Differences:

The Federalists and Alexander Hamilton believed that a body of rich and socially elite citizens should have a permanent and powerful hand in running the government.

The Republicans and Thomas Jefferson believed that government would be lasting if all of the people have a say in the democracy.

Differentiated Instruction Activity
1. Students' wording will vary. The excerpt says that the Native Americans living on the land discussed in the treaty will be allowed to continue to live on the land without being disturbed by the U.S. government or settlers. Any future land sales, however, must be made to the United States. Native Americans also agree to acknowledge the authority and protection of the U.S. government, and no other.

Answer Key

2. Students' answers will vary but should indicate some knowledge of subsequent failures of U.S. policies and actions regarding treaties with Native Americans.

Critical Thinking Skills Activity

Practicing the Skill

1. the use of dates, *two years later, soon, that same year, finally*

2. Answers may include the Northwest Territory, France and Britain, Pennsylvania, Greenville, Mississippi River, and New Orleans.

3. It gives us an idea of what is going on at the same time in different places. For instance, knowing that America was dealing with conflicts at home as well as in Europe might help us understand why Washington wanted to remain neutral.

4. 1791—conflict with Native Americans over the Northwest Territory; westward expansion

1793—American loyalties become divided over the war between the British and the French

5. Treaty of Greenville

Applying the Skill

1791: conflict over Northwest Territory

1793: Americans divided in their loyalties over the war between the British and French

1794: Whiskey Rebellion, destruction of American settlements west of Appalachia; British attempt to control the west

1795: Treaty of Greenville, Pinckney's Treaty

Geography and History Activity

1. St. Clair attempted to establish a peaceful relationship between the settlers and the Native Americans.

2. The Treaty of Greenville restricted Native American lands to only the northwestern corner of modern-day Ohio.

3. Answers will vary. Students might suggest that river locations offered transportation for American troops and supplies. The same waterways also were used by British and Native Americans, so the forts could help control the movement of the enemy.

4. Fort Detroit and Fort Miami

5. Answers may include that the Native Americans ignored the treaty because they believed the land belonged to them in the first place. They had nothing to gain from honoring the treaty.

Linking Past and Present Activity

1. Washington hired Pierre-Charles L'Enfant, an architect, to design the plan for the nation's capital.

2. L'Enfant took too much control of the project, going ahead with plans without proper authorization to do so.

3. City planners have had to provide for automobiles (adding highways and expressways) and for mass transit (adding a subway system).

4. Answers will vary, but students may conclude that the Founders were proud of their country and had grand visions of what it could become. They wanted a capital that reflected their optimism.

5. Answers will vary. Possible reasons include a sense of national pride and the city's symbolism of Americans' freedom and self-government.

Time Line Activity

1. In 1793, Washington proclaimed neutrality.

2. John Jay

3. 1796

4. the XYZ Affair

Answer Key

School-to-Home Connection Activity

What Do You Know?

Sample answers:

Partner's answer: Washington, D.C., was selected as the nation's new capital in order to win support from the Southern states for Hamilton's plan to pay off state debts.

Student's answer: Pinckney's Treaty was a treaty with Spain that gave the Americans free navigation of the Mississippi River and the right to trade at New Orleans.

Partner's answer: The British would capture American ships and impress the crews, or force the crews into the British navy.

Student's answer: The Virginia and Kentucky Resolutions claimed that the Alien and Sedition Acts violated the Constitution.

Understanding the Essential Questions

Sample answers:

1. Statement: Washington established some precedents as the first president of the United States.

Executive Branch	Separation of Powers
• established presidential authority over the executive branch	• Congress proposes the laws; the president approves or vetoes them
• established the cabinet—the heads of the State Department, the Department of the Treasury, the Department of War, and the attorney general; the president could dismiss cabinet members without congressional approval	• president concentrates on foreign affairs and military matters

2. Statement: The United States faced several challenges during Washington's administration.

Challenge	Washington's Response
American farmers violently protested the whiskey tax in the Whiskey Rebellion.	With his advisers, he decided to crush the challenge, sending the message that the government would use force when necessary to maintain social order.
Native Americans, the French, and the British fought America's westward expansion.	Washington sent troops to challenge Native American demands, and they surrendered most of what is now Ohio to the United States in the Treaty of Greenville.
France and Great Britain both tried to force the United States to join their side in the war. They captured American ships and interfered with trade, and the British impressed, or forced, American sailors into their navy.	Washington sent John Jay to Great Britain and Thomas Pinckney to Spain to negotiate treaties with those countries.

Answer Key

3. Statement: The Federalist and Republican Parties formed because there were major disagreements about important issues.

	The Federalists	The Republicans
Who led the party?	Washington and Hamilton	Jefferson and Madison
What type of government did they support?	supported a strong federal government	wanted to limit the government's power
What was their view regarding implied powers?	believed the federal government was able to use implied powers that were not expressly forbidden in the Constitution	believed that implied powers are limited to powers that are "absolutely necessary" to carry out the expressed powers stated in the Constitution
What was their view of the people's role?	supported representative government, in which elected officials ruled in the people's name	believed public office should be held by ordinary people

Reteaching Activity

1. Jefferson and the Republicans
2. Jefferson and the Republicans
3. Hamilton and the Federalists
4. Hamilton and the Federalists
5. Hamilton and the Federalists
6. Jefferson and the Republicans
7. Hamilton and the Federalists
8. Hamilton and the Federalists
9. Hamilton and the Federalists
10. Jefferson and the Republicans
11. Hamilton and the Federalists
12. Jefferson and the Republicans
13. Jefferson and the Republicans

Guided Reading Activity

The First President

1. Congress established the State Department, the Department of the Treasury, and the Department of War.
2. The Judiciary Act of 1789 established a federal court system with 13 district courts and three circuit courts.
3. The purpose of the Bill of Rights' is to protect the rights of individual liberty and the rights of people accused of crimes.

4. Hamilton planned for the federal government to pay off the debts owed by the Confederation government to other countries and to individual American citizens.
5. A bond is a paper note promising to repay borrowed money in a certain length of time.
6. If Southern leaders voted for Hamilton's plan, he would then support locating the nation's capital in the South.
7. Jefferson and Madison believed that a national bank would benefit the wealthy and that the bank was unconstitutional.

Early Challenges

1. Whiskey Rebellion
2. Native Americans
3. Anthony Wayne
4. Fallen Timbers
5. Greenville
6. neutrality
7. impressment
8. Jay's
9. Pinckney's
10. Mississippi
11. New Orleans

Answer Key

The First Political Parties

I. A. Federalists
   B. Republicans
   C. strict
   D. Federalists; Republicans

II. A. XYZ affair
   B. Alien and Sedition
   C. nullify
   D. states' rights

The Jefferson Era

Content Vocabulary Activity

1. neutral rights
2. frigate
3. secede
4. judicial review
5. tribute
6. embargo
7. Conestoga wagon
8. impressment
9. laissez-faire
10. nationalism
11. privateer
12. customs duties

Academic Vocabulary Activity

A. Word Meaning

1. alike
2. disagreement
3. power
4. sale
5. respond
6. limit
7. place a low value
8. intention

B. Word Family

1. authorize, authorized, authorizing
2. react, reacted, reacting
3. conflict(s)
4. purchase, purchased, purchasing
5. restriction(s)
6. underestimate, underestimation
7. debate, debated, debating

Primary Source Readings

1. Americans change from one administration to the next in a peaceful way without confusion, villainy, or bloodshed.
2. Jefferson gave his speech using elegant language. His manner was mild yet firm.
3. Smith approved of Jefferson's speech, because she likes its correct principles, liberal sentiments, and benevolent wishes.
4. Onlookers might have doubted Jefferson's integrity and talents, but Smith says that this speech ended their doubts.
5. Inaugural speeches take place in both. However, Jefferson was inaugurated in the Senate chamber in the morning. Today, presidential inaugurations take place outdoors in front of the Capitol and begin at noon.

Writing Skills Activity

Practicing the Skill

1. a battle during the War of 1812
2. Answers will vary. Sample answers include:
   hear—bombs bursting
   see—rocket's red glare, the flag flying
   taste—accept any reasonable answer
   touch—accept any reasonable answer
   smell—dew at dawn, gunpowder
3. Answers will vary. Sample answers include:
   Alliteration—rockets red, bombs bursting, star-spangled
   Rhyme—light and fight, gleaming and streaming, air and there, wave and brave

Answer Key

Applying the Skill

Check students' Self-Assessment Checklists. Poems should be about a personal experience and include descriptive language and imagery. It should be clear that the students revised their poems and chose their words carefully.

Social Studies Skills Activity

Practicing the Skill

1. The flowchart shows events that took place in the War of 1812 between Britain and the United States.
2. The sequence of events follows from top to bottom and is directed by arrows.
3. The British are defeated at Lake Erie.
4. General Hull led the American army into Canada.

Applying the Skill

Students' flowcharts will vary but should include logical steps to obtaining either a library card, a photo identification card, or a passport.

Differentiated Instruction Activity

1. A poultice is a kind of soft, thick paste applied to injuries. Birch, carrots, elm, and yarrow were used to make poultices.
2. Students' answers will vary. Possible answer: Doctors were scarce on the frontier, and pioneers had to use whatever was at hand that might help.

Critical Thinking Skills Activity

Practicing the Skill

1. Jefferson wanted to tell them what they should observe and report on during their expedition.
2. Jefferson seems most concerned with finding a water route across North America to the Pacific. Such a route would link the entire nation together and establish trade and transportation across the continent.

3. It is apparent that Jefferson knows the territory is already inhabited because he tells Lewis and Clark to become acquainted with the different Native American groups.
4. He seems eager to learn more about them. He asks Lewis and Clark to find out specific information about the Native Americans in the area, and he instructs Lewis and Clark to arrange visits with U. S. government officials for any Native American chiefs who would like to have such meetings.

Applying the Skill

1. A
2. D
3. D

Geography and History Activity

1. The Missouri is nicknamed "Big Muddy" because it is a powerful river with swift currents that carry great amounts of sediment and debris.
2. The expedition encountered raging currents, collapsing riverbanks, sandbars, and trees, brush, and vines.
3. Curves would have added to the length of the journey and increased the time it took to navigate the river.
4. the Yellowstone River
5. The map shows that the routes of Lewis and Clark and Zebulon Pike started on the Missouri River in or near St. Louis, Missouri.

Linking Past and Present Activity

Countries include Morocco, Algeria, Tunisia, and Libya; cities include Casablanca, Algiers, Tunis, and Tripoli.

Answer Key

Time Line Activity

EXPLORING WEST OF THE MISSISSIPPI

November 1806 Zebulon Pike first sees Pikes Peak

November 1805 The expedition reaches the Pacific Ocean

May 1804 Lewis and Clark set out from St. Louis, Missouri

October 1805 Lewis and Clark cross the Rocky Mountains

September 1806 Lewis and Clark return to St. Louis

Jan. 1804	June 1804	Jan. 1805	June 1805	Jan. 1806	June 1806

January 1804 Haiti is declared independent

May 1804 Napoleon names himself emperor of France

June 1805 A treaty ends the war with Tripoli

March 1806 Napoleon's brother is proclaimed king of Naples

EVENTS OCCURRING ELSEWHERE

School-to-Home Connection Activity

What Do You Know?

Sample answers:

Partner's answer: The Twelfth Amendment states that the presidential and vice-presidential candidates must be on separate ballots. Congress passed the amendment so there could never be another tie vote between the candidates.

Student's answer: Napoleon wanted to control territory in America by establishing a naval base on the Caribbean island of Santo Domingo, but the enslaved people revolted and threw the French out. This prevented Napoleon from establishing a naval base and led to the sale of the Louisiana Territory to the United States.

Partner's answer: The Embargo Act banned imports from all foreign nations so that Americans would not go through other countries to trade with Britain and France indirectly.

Student's answer: The War Hawks took over the Republican Party after the War of 1812.

Understanding the Essential Questions

Sample answers:

1. Statement: Thomas Jefferson and the Republicans limited the powers of the government in several ways.

They reduced military size and spending.	They repealed all federal internal taxes. They only raised government funds through taxes on imported goods and from the sale of western lands.	They did not hire a lot of people to work in the government, keeping the government small.

Answer Key

2. Statement: The Louisiana Purchase affected the nation's economy and politics.

Ways It Affected the Economy	Ways It Affected Politics
• It secured the trade route along the Mississippi River. • It provided cheap, abundant land for farming. • It inspired scientific exploration and westward expansion.	• The Constitution said nothing about buying land, but Jefferson decided the government's treaty-making powers allowed the purchase of the new territory. • Federalists worried that states formed in the territory would be Republican, so they made plans to secede.

3. Statement: There were several challenges to the nation's stability during the late 1700s and early 1800s.

Threats to Trade	Tensions in the West	War Hawks' Demands
• Barbary pirates interfered with trade and demanded tribute to let American ships pass safely. When the United States refused to pay more, it led to war. • The war between the British and French interfered with American trade. • The British were seizing American ships and impressing crews into the British navy. • The trade bans by the United States wiped out all U.S. commerce.	• White settlers were taking over more Native American land. • Native Americans formed a Confederacy and allied with the British to try to stop American settlers from taking their lands.	• Demanded that the United States go to war against Britain. • Driven by desire for land in Canada and Florida. • Wanted to expand the nation's power.

4. Statement: The United States benefited from its victory in the War of 1812.

It ended the threat of a Native American confederacy. The United States gained Native American lands from the Creek.	America earned respect from other nations.	Americans felt a new sense of patriotism and developed a strong national identity.

Reteaching Activity

1. Lewis & Clark expedition
2. Battle of Horseshoe Bend
3. war with Tripoli
4. Twelfth Amendment
5. Battle of Fort McHenry
6. Embargo Act
7. Tecumseh's confederacy
8. War of 1812
9. Louisiana Purchase

Guided Reading Activity

The Republicans Take Power

1. The candidates and their supporters sent letters to leading citizens and newspapers to publicize their views.

2. Congress passed the Twelfth Amendment to prevent another tie between a presidential and vice-presidential candidate.

3. Jefferson believed a large federal government threatened liberty, and its power and

Answer Key

size should be reduced. The states could better protect freedom.

4. The Judiciary Act of 1801 set up regional courts for the United States.

5. John Adams and John Marshall made the appointments for almost all of the judicial positions with the approval of the Federalist-controlled Congress.

6. Marshall said that the Constitution did not give the Supreme Court jurisdiction to decide Marbury's case.

7. (1) The Constitution is the supreme law. (2) The Constitution must be followed when any other law conflicts with it. (3) The judicial branch must uphold the Constitution and nullify unconstitutional laws.

The Louisiana Purchase

I. **A.** rifles [or axes]; axes [or rifles]
B. Louisiana Territory
C. New Orleans
D. Napoleon Bonaparte
E. Santo Domingo

II. **A.** treaties
B. Northwest Passage
C. Lewis; Clark
D. Sacagawea
E. Zebulon Pike
F. secede

A Time of Conflict

1. tribute
2. Tripoli
3. neutral rights
4. impressed
5. *Chesapeake*
6. Embargo Act
7. restrictions
8. Tecumseh
9. William Henry Harrison
10. Battle of Tippecanoe
11. War Hawks
12. nationalism

The War of 1812

1. F. The United States army was small and the state militias were poorly trained when war began.
2. T.
3. F. Andrew Jackson's forces defeated the Creeks at the Battle of Horseshoe Bend.
4. F. Francis Scott Key wrote "The Star-Spangled Banner" while watching bombs burst over Fort McHenry in Baltimore.
5. T.
6. F. The Treaty of Ghent did not mention the impressment of American sailors.
7. T.

Growth and Expansion

Content Vocabulary Activity

1. factory system
2. turnpike
3. sectionalism
4. free enterprise
5. cotton gin
6. American system
7. census
8. patent
9. canal
10. capitalism
11. state sovereignty
12. interchangeable parts
13. lock
14. capital

Academic Vocabulary Activity

A. Word Meaning

1. F	3. E	5. B
2. A	4. C	6. D

B. Word Usage

1. inhibit	3. conceal	5. moderate
2. sum	4. map	6. exterior

Answer Key

C. Word Family

1. verb
2. noun
3. verb, adjective
4. noun
5. adjective
6. verb
7. adjective
8. noun
9. noun
10. adjective
11. adjective
12. noun
13. adjective

Primary Source Readings

1. The author describes ordinary people such as the farmer, the mother and her children, aged parents, and the merchant, all of whom are living comfortable lives.

2. The author predicts that, if the factory closed, the farmer, mother, and merchant all would agree that their lives were much more difficult.

3. Every man should see for himself what happens when a factory closes.

4. Auto manufacturers might approve of a protective tariff, because they would not have to compete with the cheaper prices of imports and could charge more for their cars. However, American consumers might oppose the same tariff, because it would mean that American cars are more expensive to buy.

Writing Skills Activity

Practicing the Skill

1. (a) This sentence mentions that the person is a blacksmith.

2. (b) and (c) These sentences explain that the blacksmith can make and repair items, and work with wrought iron.

3. (d) This skill has no bearing on the job. It is extra information customers do not need to know.

Applying the Skill

Check students' Self-Assessment Checklist. Answers will vary, but should describe the job and list experiences and skills. Sample answer: Person needed to manage new factory. Must be able to manage people and maintain schedule. Responsible for hiring workers and fixing machines. Proven leadership skills required. Experience in textiles or heavy farming a plus.

Social Studies Skills Activity

Practicing the Skill

Students are to write one fact about each form of transportation. Students' answers will vary but could include the following:

- Rivers: The invention of steamboats made transporting goods upstream faster.
- Canal: Goods could be shipped by barge from New York City to the Great Lakes.
- Corduroy Roads: Roads were built from logs to span muddy terrain.
- Turnpikes: Travelers had to pay to use these roads built by private companies.

Applying the Skill

Students are to create a web diagram of U.S. foreign affairs policies and agreements after the War of 1812. Students' answers will vary but could include the following:

- 1817 Rush-Bagot Treaty: United States and Britain agreed to limit the number of naval vessels each could have on the Great Lakes.
- Convention of 1818: Agreement set the boundary line between United States and Canada.
- Adams-Onís Treaty: United States gained East Florida from Spain.
- Monroe Doctrine: United States issued a statement to end future European colonization in North and South America.

Differentiated Instruction Activity

1. The United States would consider dangerous any attempt by a European country to influence any countries in the Western Hemisphere; America will not meddle with existing European colonies in the

Answer Key

region; the United States would consider European interference in any independent Western Hemisphere nation to be threatening and provocative.

2. European nations are reassured that the United States will not interfere in their regional colonies. A distinction is thus made between colonies (in which European nations have a valid interest) and independent countries (in which Europe has no legitimate interest).

Critical Thinking Skills Activity

Practicing the Skill

1. The subject of the excerpt is the opposition of the United States to European influence in the Western Hemisphere.

2. The United States would consider dangerous any attempt by a European country to influence any countries in the Western Hemisphere. The United States will not meddle with existing European colonies in the region. The United States would consider European interference with any independent nation in the Western Hemisphere to be a threat.

3. First, President Monroe states his opposition to European control in the region, and then he reassures European countries that the United States will not interfere with their regional colonies. Monroe therefore makes a distinction between colonies in which European nations have a valid interest and independent countries in which European nations have no legitimate interest.

Applying the Skill

1. B   2. D   3. B

Geography and History Activity

1. Lake of the Woods

2. Owning Oregon Country would give the United States access to the Pacific Ocean.

3. Missouri and Louisiana were the two most Western states in 1824.

4. Gaining the Mexican territories meant the western border of the United States was the Pacific Ocean rather than along territory held by a foreign power.

5. The northern border was gained through peaceful negotiations with Britain; establishing the southwestern border involved military conflict with Mexico.

Linking Past and Present Activity

Students should complete the lab activity report before they answer the question. Students will discover that the ice cube with dirt packed around it will take the longest time to melt. The dirt, like the sawdust used by Wyeth and Tudor, acts as an insulator.

Time Line Activity

1. Cotton production was 100 times greater in 1820 than in 1790.

2. the cotton gin, the mechanized cotton mill, and the factory system

3. 12 years

4. the Erie Canal and the National Road

School-to-Home Connection Activity

What Do You Know?

Sample answers:

Partner's answer: A patent gives inventors the sole legal right to the invention and its profits for a certain period of time.

Student's answer: The major elements of free enterprise are competition, profit, private property, and economic freedom.

Partner's answer: Robert Fulton developed a steamboat with a powerful engine that greatly improved the transport of goods and passengers along major rivers.

Student's answer: The Supreme Court case, *Gibbons* v. *Ogden*, established that states could not enact legislation that would interfere with congressional power over interstate commerce.

Answer Key

Copyright © Glencoe/McGraw-Hill, a division of The McGraw-Hill Companies, Inc.

Understanding the Essential Questions

Sample answers:

1. Statement: The Industrial Revolution affected the U.S. economy.

Before the Industrial Revolution	After the Industrial Revolution
Most people worked in homes or workshops.	Many people moved to cities to work in the factories.
People made the things they needed by hand.	Machines were invented that allowed goods to be mass produced.
Businesses were small.	People invested money in new businesses that grew into large corporations. Free enterprise and capitalism thrived.

2. Statement: Land and water transportation affected westward expansion in several ways.

Improvement		How It Affected Transportation
More roads were built and improved, including toll roads and a national road to the West.	⟹	made it easier to travel west; provided more routes to ship goods for trade
The steamboat was developed.	⟹	improved transportation of goods and passengers along major inland rivers; made it cheaper and faster to ship goods; contributed to the growth of river cities in the West
The Erie Canal and other canals were constructed.	⟹	tied waterways together; made it cheaper and faster to ship goods; brought prosperity to cities along canal routes; linked regions together

3. Statement: Nation-building issues were resolved in the early 1800s in several ways.

Issue: Sectional differences became more intense over the issue of allowing slavery in new states.	**Issue:** Conflicts arose regarding states' rights and the federal government.	**Issue:** Territorial issues with European nations, particularly Britain and Spain, developed.
Resolution: The Missouri Compromise admitted Missouri to the United States as a slave state and Maine as a free state. It also banned slavery in the rest of the Louisiana Territory north of the 36° 30′N parallel.	**Resolution:** The Supreme Court ruled that state governments could not interfere with the federal government when the federal government was using its constitutional powers. This decision strengthened the power of the federal government over state governments.	**Resolution:** Treaties with Britain and Spain settled territorial disputes. The Monroe Doctrine limited further European colonization of North and South America.

Reteaching Activity

1. Adams-Onís Treaty
2. factory system
3. Missouri Compromise
4. cotton gin
5. turnpikes
6. Rush-Bagot Treaty
7. patents
8. *Clermont*
9. capitalism

Answer Key

10. interchangeable parts
11. Monroe Doctrine
12. canals

Guided Reading Activity

Economic Growth

1. First, poor soil in New England made farming difficult. Second, rivers and streams provided waterpower needed to run factory machines. Third, New England was close to natural resources, such as iron and coal. Fourth, the region had many ports through which goods could be shipped.

2. Interchangeable parts could be put together quickly, made machine repair easier, allowed for large-scale production of different kinds of goods, and reduced prices of goods.

3. A patent gives an inventor the sole legal right to the invention and its profits for a certain time period.

4. In the factory system, all manufacturing steps are brought together in one place to increase efficiency.

5. The terms *capitalism* and *free enterprise* describe the economy of the United States.

6. The major elements of free enterprise are competition, profit, private property, and economic freedom.

7. These people invested their money hoping to earn profits if the businesses succeeded.

8. Many cities developed along waterways so that factories could use water for power and for shipping their goods to markets.

Westward Bound

I. A. census
    B. turnpikes
    C. national road
    D. north; south
    E. steamboats
II. A. De Witt Clinton
    B. Erie Canal
    C. locks
III. A. states
    B. rivers

Unity and Sectionalism

1. Good Feelings
2. sectionalism
3. internal
4. John C. Calhoun
5. sovereignty
6. Daniel Webster
7. Henry Clay
8. American System
9. Missouri Compromise
10. Canada
11. Adams-Onís
12. Monroe Doctrine